NUMEROLOGY FOR BEGINNERS

Learn How to Use Numerology, Astrology, Numbers, and Tarot to Take Charge of Your Life and Create the One You Deserve (2022 Guide for Beginners)

Harper Horton

TABLE OF CONTENT

INTRODUCTION

Numerology began as a divination method largely practiced by pagans, but it has since gained popularity and intrigue among many people. Many individuals turn to numbers as a way to learn what is in store for them for that day, much like people rush to their horoscopes to understand what they are destined for daily.

You'll quickly understand that numbers are present everywhere in our contemporary society when you start to use numerology to learn more about your destiny. Numbers are present everywhere, from our birth dates to our phone numbers to the way we count abundance using financial values. Your birth date and name are the two numbers that are most important to focus on while trying to read your future through numbers. By solving a few simple mathematical equations, you can figure out how to obtain your numbers, which can teach you more about who you are, reveal your inclinations, and suggest methods to enjoy this human experience even more.

Numerology is a great tool to use to understand how you can grow as a person, what patterns to watch out for, and what intrinsic qualities you can tap into to help you uncover your greatest self, just like any other technique of this kind.

You will learn how numerology influences you, what you can learn about yourself based on your numbers, and how to use numerology to co-create the life of your dreams in this book. You will discover that by drawing on all of this information, you have access to a completely new level of understanding of both yourself and the world around you. Prepare to have your mind completely blown as you come to realize how simple and accurate everything is at the same time.

I've listed a few chapter summaries below to give you an idea of what to anticipate.

You will learn about the lengthy and varied history of numerology in Part 1's Chapters 1 through 5, as well as how it affects people.

To start getting a sense of how your chart appears, you will also learn how to find your numbers using these ancient concepts. You'll learn how unique you are by using this advice to make your very own chart.

You will discover the meaning of these numbers and how to interpret them for your chart in Part 2 for Chapters 6 through 15.

You will learn more about your life and destiny routes as well as the traits that, according to your numbers, you are most likely to identify with. This will also assist you in identifying more significant information, such as your areas of strength and weakness, and suggestions for enhancing your general sense of wellbeing.

You will learn how numerology fits into various divination reading techniques in Part 3 for Chapters 16 through 19, how to use numerology in daily life, and how to use numerology to enhance your intuitive abilities. It will be a great chance for you to switch from utilizing numerology to better understand who you are to using it to make your life better in general. You can get the most out of your numerology experience in this way.

As you read this book, I hope you will realize exactly how amazing this divination tool is and how beautiful it may be to use in your life. The moment is now to start learning about and applying numerology if you are ready to do so. Since there is a lot to learn and you want the learning experience to be exciting, be sure to take your time and enjoy the process. Enjoy yourselves!

PART 1
UNDERSTANDING NUMBERS

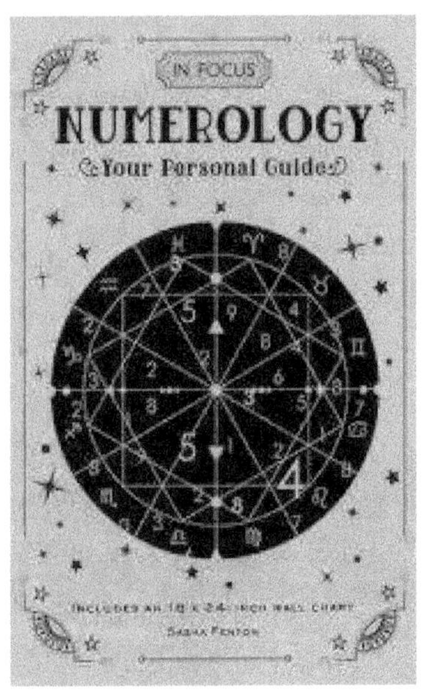

CHAPTER 1

The Importance of Numbers

There are several reasons why numbers are important. In our daily lives, there are numerous ways to track things using numbers. We use numbers in a variety of ways, including tracking the amount of money in our bank accounts, the number on our bank cards, our phone numbers and social security numbers, in our line queue numbers, and many other places. We are in constant contact with numbers because we are almost constantly counting something or being counted by something.

Although many may view this as nothing more than a counting system, many others think that these numbers have great significance and were not randomly selected for us but rather by destiny. Understanding the importance of numerology and incorporating it into your daily life can help you gain a better understanding of yourself and your experiences, which can aid in broadening your perspective and increasing your sense of self-awareness.

How Does Numerology Work?
Numerology is regarded as a divine correlation between numbers and the occurrences of worldly events that we encounter on Earth. Numerology is regarded as an occult science that aids people in predicting events on Earth based on the numbers about those circumstances, including those involving careers, finances, relationships, and even one's health. Receiving them is seen as a favorable omen that assures you that something good is on the way, as some people even think that you can anticipate a miracle or a good blessing based on the alignment of these numbers.

Why Is Numerology Used by People?

People have developed a liking for numbers because they believe they are a potent means of communication and connection with the invisible.

Using numerology can be a terrific way to communicate back and forth with that entity, whether you believe in God, the Universe, a Source, a Higher Power, or an unnamed larger presence. The energy connected to your karmic destiny on Earth, your life path, and your teachings may all be found via numerology. The ability to make decisions that are more in line with their genuine purpose in life feels like a strong opportunity for many people now that they have access to this knowledge. Numerology is valuable to many more people since it helps them feel as though they have a real-life purpose, which allows them to start creating in line with it. In this way, kids transition from feeling lost and confused while roaming to strolling confidently in the direction of everything that feels right for them.

Numerology is valued and beloved by many people for several reasons, including the fact that it is a part of a wide range of belief systems. Numerology has been utilized in one form or another by numerous religions and cultures as a means of establishing significance through the worth of numbers. Numerology is a flexible divination method that allows a wide range of people to utilize it to connect with the divine without feeling as though they are going against their religious beliefs. Christians, for instance, are permitted to use numerology because it is mentioned in the Bible, but they are not permitted to use Tarot cards because their religion considers them to be witchcraft.

Many individuals can start to understand themselves more thoroughly without feeling terrible or wrong for what they are doing thanks to the availability of a divination instrument that is so generally recognized by almost every religious background out there. This makes numerology not only a useful tool but also an intriguing one because of how adaptable it is and how many other unaccepting belief systems accept it. Numerology is a good alternative for those who are interested in divination and who wish to use a divination instrument without betraying their religion.

Finally, the fact that numbers are thought to have been the Universe's primordial form makes them important. Almost everything in the universe can be reduced to a numerical number, which explains why science and physics are such well-liked academic fields for learning about Earth and life in general. Given that everything can be reduced to a number and that they are so frequently employed, numerology is not only one of the most generally used tools, but also one of the most adaptable in terms of what it may be used for.

Numerology enables you to gain insight into a variety of topics, including your future, your compatibility with other people and situations, and even which circumstances are ideal for you. Additionally, numerology can improve your ability to converse with the Universe or the higher force you believe in. Due to its incredible potential, numerology is considered to be a divination method that everyone can benefit from knowing about and applying to their daily life. Numerology might be a terrific opportunity for you to gain that if you have been yearning for something deeper or greater in your life.

The Workings of Numerology
Three numbers in particular will have the greatest meaning for you personally when it comes to numerology. Your psychic number, destiny number, and name number are three of these numbers. Your psychic number is a reflection of your perspective on yourself or the

filter through which you view yourself. Through your psychic number, you can discover more about your character, how your personality changes over time, and how you tend to interact in daily life. Chapter 3 has more information on your psychic number.

Your destiny number might help you figure out what it is you came to Earth to learn and what you will do during your time here. Knowing your destiny number can help you identify your life's mission and open up the possibility of learning how to carry it out. Additionally, you will discover what your life lessons are based on your destiny number. This information can help you better understand what you may encounter in life and how to approach it with a greater sense of awareness and preparedness.

Your name number influences how you will interact with other people in general as well as how you will build relationships with them. You can learn more about your social identity by using the name number, which is essentially your social number.
Your name and name number can both change over time, which means that you can develop different aspects of your identity through these changes.

Your whole chart will be created once you have determined for yourself what these three numbers are. In this way, you may start utilizing these numbers to gain a deeper understanding of who you are and to create an awareness of how you can move through life more in tune with who you are. Many people find that having access to this information acts as a guide for how they can move on with decisions, life changes, and major life advancements, and you might discover that it does the same for you!

CHAPTER 2

The History of Numerology

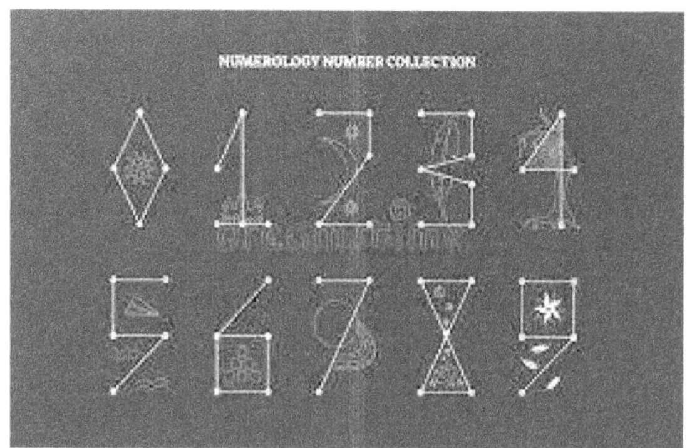

It is well known that each number carries a vibration or energy of its own. Every number has its vibration, according to those who study numerology, and we may use these vibrations to help us identify significant information about people, places, things, and events. These frequencies are comparable to the energy that new-age believers assert is shared by crystals, gemstones, colors, and essential oils.

Numerology itself has several different lines of origin that can be used to pinpoint the origins of various numerological systems. Although Pythagoras is considered to be the founder of numerology, other periods of history have also employed divination techniques that are similar to numerology. Below, we'll look at a couple of them.

Using The Original Numerology and Pythagoras
While there are a few various theories concerning the origins of numerology, the one that is most widely acknowledged is that Pythagoras, a Greek philosopher who was born in Greece about 569

B.C., is where it all began. Even though we do not have a lot of knowledge about Pythagoras or his work, there is still enough information about it to be able to appreciate what he accomplished to advance numerology. Some historians contend that Pythagoras himself owned the knowledge, but that his students assembled the knowledge that is presently known as a result of his labor.

According to Pythagoras' teachings, numerology was regarded as a technique where you would find numbers and then use your imagination to assign meaning to them. For these linkages or meanings to be noticed, you need ideally to use your mind to study them. In other words, he thought we needed to assign meaning to these numbers and that they had been set as tools or divine direction for us to employ on our journeys. This implied that employing numerology for divinity was a two-way exchange of information: the divine placed the numbers there for us, and we assigned them significance.

Numerology will probably be rejected as a divination method because many people will seek to explain the location of the numbers as a mere coincidence rather than something that was put there specifically for us. As a result, these people will probably reject numerology's significance and opt to think that the numbers are random and that we are being overly sensitive to think that they have any significance beyond the number's literal meaning.

Christian Number Theory
Traditional numerology is disapproved of by Christianity because it is seen to be a kind of divination similar to tarot or astrology. The "Jesus number" and other sacred numbers that have persisted throughout history do appear in a variety of numerology in the sacred writings, nevertheless. Therefore, despite the possibility that

conventional numerology readings like the ones we are considering in this book will be disregarded, the reality of approved sacred numbers, angel numbers, and the Jesus number still exist. This indicates that there is still a branch of numerology that Christians can employ to benefit their lives without compromising their beliefs.

Applied Numerology

Numerology has changed a little since Pythagoras' day. Today, as our understanding of divination has evolved, people like Ruth A. Drayer, Mrs. L. Dow Balliett, Juno Jordan, Florence Campbell, Lynn Buess, Mark Gruner, Faith Javane, Dusty Bunker, and Kathleen Roquemore are credited with developing modern reading techniques. Each of these people has studied classical numerology and has created their research based on what they have learned, which is normally where all contemporary numerology interpretations and understandings have come from.

The likelihood is that if you are learning numerology today, you are doing so through an instructional approach that was modified from the old reading method by one of these numerologists. Even yet, it can still be referred to as a classic reading technique because it's possible that your reading habits haven't changed significantly over time. To maintain as true to the traditional reading manner as feasible, we are applying a combination of modern understandings in this book.

CHAPTER 3

Your Psychic Number

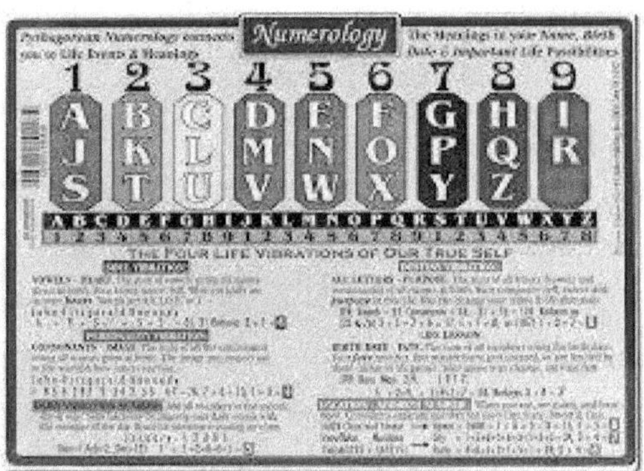

According to numerology, your psychic number, which was previously discussed, will assist you to decide how you would view yourself. This score indicates how you see your personality, character, and ultimately, who you are as a person. Having access to this number can help you learn more about your fundamental characteristics and how you view the world so that you can acquire a more profound grasp of who you are as a person.

Understanding Your Psychic Number

Similar to your astrological sign, your psychic number is the one that, according to numerology, speaks the most about who you are. You will gain important knowledge about yourself and how you present yourself to the outside world from this. Understanding this number helps you better understand your personality, how you interact with the world, and how others are most likely to perceive you.

When you read about your psychic number in part 2 after learning it, you'll probably have a strong connection to what it implies. In part

2, you'll learn how your psychic number affects your personality, how to identify your strengths and weaknesses using this number, and how to use this number to find your balance. Knowing this number will not only help you gain a better understanding of who you are, but it will also show you how to approach decisions and other life events in a way that genuinely suits your personality.

For instance, because 1 is the number of independence and 6 is the number of harmony and caregiving, a person with the psychic number 1 and a person with the psychic number 6 are likely to approach life in quite different ways. Therefore, a person with a number 1 would be more likely to base their decision on themselves and their own needs, whereas a person with a number 6 would be more likely to focus their decision on the needs of those around them. You must try to use this number to better understand both the essence of who you are as a person and how you can grow as a person, as well as yourself. This in-depth comprehension will show you how to live more easily and either co-create or manifest a life experience that is more in line with your goals.

By doing this, you may stop attempting to live your life according to other people's advice, which may not even be beneficial to you, and start living your life according to what benefits you. In a way, being aware of this number might assist you in permitting yourself necessary to become who you truly are and adopt your philosophy of life.

Find Your Psychic Number: A Guide
Your birth date, which is a number that cannot be changed in this lifetime, serves as the foundation for your psychic number. You can determine your psychic number by multiplying your birth date by

one until you get a single number or a master number, which is a double-digit number that keeps repeating (i.e. 11, 22, 33.)
Here is an illustration of this equation:
Date of Birth: June 10, 1983
(Day) 10 numbers
Formula: 1+0 Equals 1.
Spiritual Number: 1

CHAPTER 4

Your Name, Your Number

Your name number is a reflection of how you relate to others and how they relate to you. Pay close attention to this number because it has a lot to do with how you can connect with those around you. Through it, you can learn about the patterns that you are probably going to use in all of your relationships as well as how your relationships will develop. You may improve your capacity to connect with people in a better way and create relationships in general by becoming more conscious of these inherent tendencies.

It is crucial to understand that your name number may change as a result of name changes made over your lifetime, such as getting married and adopting a new name. Knowing this makes it easier for you to transition your consciousness whenever your name changes since it makes you aware that how you interact with people can also change.

What Your Name and Number Mean

Your name number will play a significant role in how you interact with other people. This can help you gain a deeper understanding of relationship-related topics like how you relate to others, the roles you assign them in your life, and the life cycles that your relationships often follow. You can start to comprehend why you behave the way you do in relationships, how you contribute to partnerships, and what strengths and limitations you typically carry in your relationships after you are aware of your name number.

This can reveal everything, including the reasons behind your tendency to withdraw or close off in relationships or the reasons behind your "clinginess" and tendency to form close bonds with the people in your life. The name number will be able to predict any peculiarities or inclinations you may have in your interpersonal interactions. Additionally, you will comprehend why you draw the people you do into your life as well as how others often handle and perceive you in romantic interactions. This will give you a better understanding of why people act a certain way toward you, what positive and negative traits you typically experience in relationships, and why particular traits might be present in your relationships quite frequently.

In this regard, we are discussing traits that may not entirely be your fault, such as people frequently going out of their way to be kind to you or betraying you even though they are generally kind and decent people. Your ability to recognize these relationship habits and change them will be made easier as you have a better understanding of your numerology and how it affects your relationships.

Finding Your Name and Number

Using a numerology chart, you may get your name number by looking up the corresponding number for each letter in your name and adding those numbers up until they reach a specific numerological value. There are various name charts for the various numerology systems, but the most widely used, accepted, and traditional name chart is read using a straightforward system.

The chart is shown below:
1 A, J, S,
2, B, K, T,
4, D, M, V,
5, E, N, W,
6, F, O, X,
7, G, P, Y,
8, H, Q, Z,
9, I, R

In this case, the name "Samantha Louise Smith" would be calculated as follows:
Samantha Louise Smith, a.k.a.
S=1, A=1, M=4, A=1, N=4, T=2, H=8, A=1, L=3, O=6, U=3, I=9, S=1, E=5, S=1, M=4, I=9, T=2, H=8
 are the numerical values.
Equation: 7+3   =   1   and
1+1+4+1+4+2+8+1+3+6+3+9+1+5+1+4+9+2+8 = 73
First Name Number

CHAPTER 5

Your Destiny Number

Your destiny number, which is determined by your birthday, will help you decide what you will go through in this lifetime. Since it is the most frequently spoken number in numerology, people's destiny number is frequently the first number they learn when they start using it. Since you cannot change the day that you were born, it stands to reason that your destiny number cannot be altered. Your destiny number follows you throughout the entire journey. The destiny number is also referred to as your life path number because it aids in determining your likely life path in this lifetime and provides excellent insight into what you are likely to experience and how.

Understanding Your Destiny Number

Your destiny number will reveal everything to you, including your life's purpose and the karmic patterns you are most likely to experience during your lifetime. Your destiny number can show you who is likely to cross your path, what lessons you will learn, what themes will recur throughout your life, and what difficulties you will likely encounter. You could start to feel a little astonished when you discover that your life has so far had a lot in common with your destiny number. Realizing that many of the difficulties and troubles you have encountered in life were predetermined and that this is nothing exceptional for you may even cause you to feel at ease.

Many people find it refreshing to realize that everything they are going through in life is exactly what they were supposed to go through once they realize that the fact that something has been placed in their path indicates that they were meant to experience it. As a result, if you were supposed to experience it, you were also meant to possess or acquire the courage to do so, rather than believing that there is no hope and that you will be at its mercy for the rest of your life.

Knowing your destiny number can assist you in understanding and finding peace with your life's problems and struggles as well as your sense of purpose in life. Many people may not yet fully comprehend what their life's mission is if they do not yet know their destiny number. As a result, they can be walking around aimlessly while attempting to figure out exactly what it is they are supposed to be doing with their lives. Or they can discover that they know exactly what they need to be doing but are unsure of why. You can gain a deeper knowledge of why you are here and what you are intended to do while you are here by knowing your destiny number, which can help you with these critical questions about yourself.

Find Your Destiny Number: How to Do It
By converting your full birthdate into an equation, you can discover your destiny number. Your birthday's numerical values are first identified, and they are then added together to create a single, complete number. Except when your equation yields a master number, such as 11, 22, 33, or another, in which case you should leave it alone because these numbers also have their unique significance.

Here is an illustration of the destiny number formula:
Date of birth: August 16, 2010
Data Value: August 16, 2010
Equation: 1+8 = 9; 0+8+1+6+2+0+1+0 = 18.
Goal Number: 9

PART 2:
THE PERSONALITY NUMBERS' MEANINGS

CHAPTER 6

The Independent

The energy of independence flows deeply into your numerology chart if the number one appears in your chart. Because they are the first number, ones are associated strongly with new beginnings and fresh starts. Number ones enjoy independence and new beginnings, in addition to leadership roles.

Primary Vibration

Number one is seen as having masculine energy since it thrives on independence, self-reliance, strength, and forcefulness. Number one enjoys starting fresh, coming up with new ideas, and standing out from the crowd. This energy is very uplifting and demands boldness, raw power, and power. The first vibration is well recognized for being highly instinctual and intuitive and for using these two energies to start new things in the world. The first energy in your chart represents your willingness to explore new things, break new ground, and set the pace for these brand-new beginnings. It's likely that you borrowed the concept or improved it from someone else, and now you want to guide everyone toward making this novel idea a reality.

The Psychic Number One

One energy, as a psychic number, represents a person who aspires to the position of leadership. Number one enjoys taking charge, exercising authority, and motivating groups of people to succeed in various endeavors.

They are very creative and will probably want to discover the best approach to carry out a task before advising and directing everyone else to carry out the task in the same manner so that everyone can meet their high expectations.

Those who choose occupations involving leadership will be very critical of their team because they want to believe that they are the greatest at all they do and will judge themselves based on the abilities and traits of any teams they lead. Having said that, they will typically be courteous when leading their team to victory, albeit they might not always exhibit genuine compassion. To put it another way, you might tend to act compassionately without actually feeling it to make the person you are leading feel compassionate, which will make them more likely to resume performing to a higher level. Because of this, the number one concern for the projects is not always sincere and frequently has a hidden meaning.

However, when the top performer demonstrates genuine compassion, you can bet that they are doing so to the fullest extent feasible. Because they always want to be the greatest, they will probably take extra care to listen carefully, understand your needs, and respond to you in the best way possible. This is because they want to be the most compassionate person there is.
As the first person, you probably think of yourself as being highly domineering and pushy in general. You can frequently get criticism for being pushy or for always wanting things done "your way."

Because you believe that your way is the greatest way to do things, you automatically assume that everyone else feels the same way. You could be startled to hear that others have varied preferences and that they can choose to complete tasks in alternative ways, especially if you consider those alternative methods to be inferior. It could take some time for you to realize that there are various approaches to achieving the same end and that it is OK for others to approach situations differently than you do.

You are probably well-known for being meticulous and well-organized when it comes to your style. You prefer things to be done a certain way because it makes you happy and satisfied. You want things done a certain way not only so that they appear to be done correctly in your eyes, but also because you believe that doing things this way will help you gain attention for what you have accomplished, which will make you feel very proud. You have a lot of self-confidence, which can occasionally be misconstrued as egotism or self-centeredness. You enjoy receiving praise for the work you accomplish, so you frequently go above and beyond to earn it. You then ask questions in a way that encourages praise from those around you.

Your persistent desire to be the best and win others' admiration may force you to occasionally become a people-pleaser or a perfectionist.

The number one as a name
If your name number on your chart is number one, you tend to lead in relationships in a highly masculine and leadership-focused manner. In partnerships, you prefer to take the lead and often insist on having things done your way so that you may feel confident and safe. When someone else tries to assume the role of the leader, you can feel awkward and discover that you don't get along with them. This could either result in partnerships full of toxic disputes or in you being very passive and "checking out" the connections that you are in. It is challenging for you to contribute when you feel undervalued and unwelcome in a relationship where you are not acknowledged as the leader. You could feel deeply rejected by someone else when you

take the initiative or create the foundation for the relationship. This can hurt a lot.

You enjoy seeing others smile, in part. You enjoy seeing others happy in general and in part because you enjoy how having happy connections makes you seem. When the people in your life only have nice things to say about you, it reflects well on you and makes you feel great about who you are and what you can do for the world.

 Additionally, you enjoy making suggestions for activities that can advance relationships or accomplish something major together so that you can take ownership of your relationship's success. This will give you the confidence boost you need while telling others about your news because you will ultimately receive all the credit for starting this new chapter in your relationship. Again, because you are ultimately motivated by your reputation and what other people think of you, you have a propensity to be quite shady in your relationships.

This does not necessarily imply that you are a nasty person or that you are selfish in relationships, but it does indicate that you run the risk of adopting this attitude in them. If you continue to behave in this way, you risk alienating others because they will start to see that you are only in the relationship for your self-validation. Understanding this pattern enables you to identify your motivation for having a good reputation, which you can then utilize to motivate you to keep giving while deliberately deciding to become more mindful of performing selfless acts of love and compassion.

You are enthusiastic about love, even though there are moments when it seems as though everything should revolve around you. Love makes you happy and makes you feel wonderful. It also tends to provide you with the inspiration you need to start fresh in life. You probably discover that you are the kind of person that either has intimate relationships with individuals or none at all. You dislike partial partnerships in which you are only loosely attached because they can come across as feeling incredibly fake to you. Once more, you appreciate the best of the greatest, including superior connections.

One as a Number of Destiny

A number one in your destiny number may allude to this being a lifetime filled with numerous novel experiences. Numerologists often hold that a number one destiny number indicates that you are in your first Earthly incarnation, making it possible that you are a "young soul" or a soul that has not yet reached the spiritual maturity that comes from living many lives. Numerologists claim that since you are a newcomer to this planet, almost everything you encounter will be unfamiliar to you. As a result, this lifetime is one in which you should try to expose yourself to as many novel experiences as you can.

Being the first person in your destiny means that you are quite open-minded and have a lot to learn when you arrive here. You are unlikely to be jaded about anything because you have no information lingering on a soul level, which implies you are also unlikely to have ingrained phobias from previous lives. For instance, numerologists claim that you have never had a prior life, making it improbable that you have a severe fear of fire as a result of having been burned there. Since you are less prone to be inhibited than those with other life path numbers, you are more likely to have the courage and confidence to try out all of these new activities. This may result in a strong sense of self-assurance, self-worth, and self-esteem.

The drawback of being so outgoing and self-assured is that you haven't had a lot of chances to confront and get over uncomfortable emotions, making painful situations more likely to leave a lasting impression on you.

Because you have not yet learned how to absorb the energy of these intensely painful emotions, you will probably find that anything from rejection to heartbreak feels much worse to you. Due to how powerful these emotions can be, you may experience several deeply ingrained traumas in your lifetime, which could result in you carrying these traumas forward if you do not heal them. You can avoid carrying any of your terrible experiences forward as ingrained worries in other incarnations by being very deliberate about resolving them in this lifetime.

Being on the number one destiny path has many advantages, one of which is that you probably do not carry a lot of karma with you in this lifetime.

You will have accrued any karma you are carrying on Earth during this lifetime, so you can try to neutralize it now to reduce how much you bring with you in the future. You may discover that you have gathered a lot of karma in your life if you have been toxically self-centered throughout your life thus far. Because you do not yet grasp the concept of karma, one of the drawbacks of having a number one destination path can be that you occasionally become unkind or hurtful to those around you. As a result, if you don't take the time to recognize this possible trend and attempt to balance it as you go, you can quickly build up karma. Do not worry if you have already amassed a lot of karma; you can still release it in this incarnation so that you do not carry it over into subsequent existence. Self-awareness is a huge asset for you right now.

CHAPTER 7

The Cooperative Peacemaker, Number 2

Because people with the number two energy value peace, it is referred to as the cooperative peacemaker energy. If you have a number two in your chart, it indicates that you highly value tranquility and comfort in your life and will frequently go to considerable efforts to obtain these traits. At least one aspect of your life will likely be highly essential to you, and you will probably reject any events that don't contribute to your tranquility. Let's examine some further characteristics connected to the numerological number two in more detail.

The Second Vibration

Because it is welcoming and cooperative, the number two has a highly feminine energy vibration. As long as no one takes advantage of the number two's receptivity and collaboration, they can easily experience peace and harmony in their lives by using their cooperation and receptivity to welcome these two qualities. Gentleness, kindness, justice, selflessness, intuition, composure, flexibility, and elegance are further characteristics of a number two energy. You are vibrating with an energy that is incredibly harmonious and tranquil in every aspect if you are vibrating with the energy of number two.

The Psychic Number Two

People with the number 2 as their psychic number position tend to be relatively calm people. Because they do not like conflict, they may be seen as peaceful and agreeable. A number two psychic is renowned for being kind and caring, as well as liking jobs of responsibility and service. The character of the number two personality is very mild and soft, and they frequently exhibit great flexibility and sensitivity in their daily lives. These two characteristics help individuals maintain their tranquility while experiencing things, in their opinion.

A person with psychic number 2 is kind and harmonious without losing their voice while they are vibrating in the positive two energy. They are exceptional at achieving what they want without creating too many commotions since they are skilled at efficient communication. When there is a dispute, two people can keep things under control by defusing the situation with peace and de-escalating the tension. People who try to quarrel with a number two psychic person frequently discover that they need to immediately calm down from their strong emotions to speak more logically and politely.

As joy and peace are found in life's silver linings, people with these two energy will probably discover that they tend to gravitate toward optimism and positivity frequently. They prefer to express themselves quietly and calmly, and as a result, they may occasionally come off as delicate or overwhelmingly feminine. But when two energy does become combative, do not be shocked. A pair will stand up and defend themselves if they genuinely believe their peace is being disturbed and the situation or the offender is not willing to back down. Because they do not like to live in this atmosphere, they are difficult to agitate and frequently settle back down quickly after being frustrated.

For fear of being confronted by others, a two who are residing in a negative shadow aspect of the two energy may find it difficult to speak their truth or own their experiences.
To prevent disruption in their life and avoid attracting unfavorable attention to themselves, they could downplay their own beliefs or

realities. This might cause a two energy to feel disregarded and insulted because, in their eyes, everyone should be treated with the same compassion and harmony in life, and when they are not, they feel rejected. Unfortunately, the two will rarely see that the people in their lives have learned to disregard their perspective or disregard what they have to say because of their people-pleasing tendencies. A two energy may not only remain silent when they should be speaking up but also become so helpful to others that they are exploited.

They run the risk of being given more in their employment or relationships than they can handle since they don't want to turn down opportunities or disappoint others by saying no. Additionally, to balance the situation, they may find themselves unnecessarily applauding those who have a propensity for being nasty or dramatic. To maintain control of the peace, twos have a reputation for trying to handle any situation's emotions on their own. This can result in unneeded burdens, intense suffering, and feelings of rejection when things inevitably go wrong and they blame themselves for it.

A name number two
You are a person who loves harmony and collaboration in your relationships if your name number position is a two. You enjoy being in relationships with people who share your desire for a peaceful and enjoyable life because it makes you feel at ease and relaxed. These activities keep you pretty calm, so you are quite content performing them, such as strolling through a peaceful park and feeding the ducks or relaxing on your patio with iced tea. You might find serenity by being more daring or outspoken, or you might find peace by being more reserved and introverted, depending on the other numbers in your chart.

In either case, once you have established what peace means to you, you will seek out and draw in individuals who share your preference for peace in their own life. It will be simple to attract folks who are similarly low-key and laid-back to you if you are clear on what calm looks and feels like for you.

You notice that your relationships are quite relaxed and easygoing when you are in flow with your second name number. Most likely, you don't dispute with people frequently, and you don't make room for those who do. To prevent having this drama in your space, you will promptly enforce your limits and end the relationship if someone starts to argue excessively or otherwise frequently disturbs your serenity.

Your partnership will be what some people would describe as dreamy for individuals who value serenity, like yourself. You frequently discover that both of you deeply appreciate one another and care deeply about each other's pleasure in the relationship. You enjoy socializing and receiving support and encouragement, thus it is typical for you to serve as the group's motivator. Additionally, since receiving encouragement from others makes you feel good about yourself, you may even seek it out occasionally. You are highly loyal and trustworthy in relationships, and you frequently seek out friends and lovers who are as well. As a result, neither you nor your partners need to worry about betrayal very often.

Your relationships might feel very taxing and draining if your number two name number is out of the flow. You might be manipulated into getting attached to people in toxic relationships because of how cooperative you are. Manipulative people may catch wind of your cooperative nature and use you to further their ends, rarely giving you or your needs any thought. To prevent being used for your cooperative inclinations, you will need to stay away from selfish, disrespectful people. You should exercise caution when it comes to your propensity to tone down your personality to avoid rejection or to avoid conflict.

You may prevent getting exhausted in relationships by having to put on a mask that is not authentic to who you are by owning who you are and being loyal to yourself and your opinions.

Two as a Number of Destiny

If your destiny number is two, you probably identify with concepts like empath and lightworker, which are directly related to your life's purpose. If two is your destiny number, it means you care deeply about advancing peace in the world and are likely to live your life in ways that support peace in general.

You probably embrace the underdog, care deeply about justice, and feel compelled to help others around you. You might find that you're drawn to professions like social work, volunteering, law, or therapy. You want to either fight for them or give them the resources they need to find and create peace if you want to help people.

Realizing that not everyone is as dedicated to peace as you are may force you to learn some extremely difficult lessons in life. This realization may leave you feeling deeply uneasy and hopeless. When you think about the current situation of the world, you could feel dejected or overwhelmed because you realize that there is still a lot of brutality and injustice that you find to be incomprehensible. You believe that everyone deserves equality and that we should treat each other and all other living creatures with respect. As you fight for animals' welfare as well, you might discover that you are doing more than just fighting for human peace and wellbeing. You can even advocate for a vegetarian or vegan diet to show your support because you find it difficult to accept the thought of eating an animal-based diet.

You will gain a valuable lesson on how to maintain your inner calm while showing respect for the world around you. Numerous teachings and karmic patterns will be delivered to you, aiding in your understanding of how to live in harmony with the people around you. You will learn how to express your perspective while also respecting the opinions of others, how to interact in relationships that value mutual respect, and how to defend yourself against those who lack peace without upsetting your peace.

You are learning how to participate in the collective without taking on the burden of the entire world, therefore boundaries and a willingness to recognize oneself as independent of other people are crucial.

A number two life path, according to numerologists, indicates that you are still developing spiritually and are not yet regarded as an ancient soul. Because of this, you could still find it difficult to fully comprehend Earth and the experiences you are having on Earth from a spiritual and energetic standpoint. On the one hand, you have a pure and innocent belief system that results from ignorance, much like a toddler who hasn't seen how the real world operates. On the other side, because you have been in this situation before, you can have a level of conceit that makes you believe you know more than you do. Keep yourself in check and concentrate on intentionally remaining open to the teachings that you have yet to learn on Earth by being aware of this.

CHAPTER 8:

Number 3 : The Creative and Self-Expressive

Because it is a number that flourishes in social settings, the number three is frequently called the "socialite number." Number threes have a propensity for being gregarious and vibrating at a very upbeat and outgoing level. If the number three appears in your chart, there's a good probability that you're eccentric and outgoing, and this is a core aspect of who you are. Discover more about the characteristics of the number three energy by reading on!

The Third Vibration

In contrast to the energy of the number two, the energy of the number three is much more extroverted. Number three places higher importance on creativity and self-expression than number two does on peace. A number three can be compared to an eccentric and well-educated art major who is known for being the life of the party while having cocktails at a gathering for artists. This person enjoys traveling and meeting new people since inspiration is found there. They then use their inspiration to get creative and either produce something new or add a new element to their self-expression. This song has a great sense of balance, vivacity, and humor. Since they spend so much of their time exploring and learning about the world around them to satisfy their insatiable curiosity, they are also renowned for being inventive and intelligent.

The Psychic Number Three

If your psychic number is three, you probably have a reputation for being outspoken and unusual. You can even be referred to as odd, unusual, out there, or alternative by your loved ones. You find the idea of leading a routine life uninteresting since it limits your ability to express your creativity and who you are, thus you are probably drawn to leading a special life. Your unique characteristics and the other characteristics you have in your chart will determine exactly how this appears.

One manifestation of this can be your intense drive, which leads you to start your own business and forge your route in life using your imagination and self-expression. You can be so opposed to conventional living that you go to great lengths to stand apart from the crowd. You could certainly characterize who you are and how you approach life with the label "hipster." Another way you could express yourself is by maintaining a typical life route while adding your special flair to it.

This distinctive quality could be anything, such as the way you speak, the way you share your humor or the way you present yourself each day. Because you constantly seem to be at the forefront of it all, you have a reputation for having outstanding taste and are probably responsible for introducing your pals to the newest trends in pop culture and life in general. Your insatiable curiosity keeps you interested in everything that appeals to your unique self-expression preferences, and as a result, you are constantly discovering novel concepts that you are eager to try out.

Even when these concepts are terrible, such as tie-dye overalls, you somehow manage to pull them off. You have a reputation for making the impossible happen because you can think outside the box to find a solution to almost any problem.

Since you tend to love laughter and you appreciate it much more when you can make others laugh with you, you may be also well known for your amazing sense of humor. Contrary to popular belief, you will not crack a joke solely to make other people laugh; rather, you will do so because you know it will make you laugh.

Because you are so talkative, you might discover that you exude a very youthful and occasionally even childlike vibe. Because you are so imaginative and creative, you are also recognized for having psychic talents or perhaps even being intuitive. You probably find it easy to manifest and were startled to realize that others find it more difficult because to you, it seems like a normal part of life. Making things happen with your thoughts is simple for you because you are so in touch with your mind.

The number three as a name
If your name number is three, you probably lead a very active and involved social life. Number threes are known to thrive on a high level of social connection, so you are always socializing, whether you are out with pals every night of the week or just leaving the house to chat with the barista for a little longer on your way to work. Your phone is probably ringing off the hook, or at the very least, social media is abuzz. Since you like the chance to catch up with the people you care about and converse for hours on end, likely, you do not mind phone calls nearly as much as some people appear to.

Even if you don't make a lot of phone calls, you probably still participate in several text or instant message chats simultaneously to keep your mind active.

You make a great friend when your name number three is in harmonious flow with you. You probably draw in people with a lot of energy who are known to be as extroverted as you are, and your group probably engages in all kinds of bizarre events. You might even start comparing your group to ones you watch on television, where they always seem to be getting into interesting and thrilling situations.

Because of the energy you inherently attract into your life, a normal night out at a café might turn into a crazy autobiography-worthy experience for you. For the people in your life to stick around, they either need to have as much energy as you have or they need to enjoy your high energy. If not, they won't. Your relationships are probably highly fulfilling for you, while occasionally being complicated.

In a bad flow, you could come out as loud and intimidating. This occurs when you do not surround yourself with the correct people and wind up making friends with those that do not appreciate your outspoken attitude. Your high energy may start to change into negative energy if you are surrounded by others who do not share or appreciate it. You can find yourself disagreeing with others or even doubting and bullying yourself for being terrible or incorrect for your naturally extroverted personality rather than letting your energy out and having fun and highly engaged relationships.

If you are seriously out of touch with yourself, you might even start to manipulate or be harmful in your relationships as you try to make other people more outgoing and high-spirited like you. Instead of recognizing that they are not as extroverted as you are and seeking friends or lovers who are, you could attempt harder to pressure them into changing once you understand it won't work. As you never learn to affirm yourself or permit yourself to be the loud version of yourself that you have been hiding, this can lead to a vicious cycle of self-sabotage and unhealthy relationships that do not meet your needs.

Three as a Number of Destiny
There are a lot of different things you might do in life if your destiny number is three. You can create anything you want thanks to your strong creative abilities, so it seems to reason that you will be drawn to activities or vocations that encourage original thought and self-expression. Because of how inventive they are, threes are renowned for being the world's entrepreneurs or inventors. In contrast to one energy, which will create to have solutions so that they may be the best, threes produce to express themselves and create, thus they are not scared to come off as stupid.

Because of this, a three energy will constantly be creating new things and attempting new endeavors without letting failures or unfavorable results stop them. Regardless matter how many times they have failed at this endeavor, they will keep creating and strive to share their works with the world. The most popular profession choices for creative number threes are intuitive ones like being psychics or life coaches, as well as artistic, musical, fashion-related, and other careers that allow for creative expression.

The difficulties in life that the number three encounters are frequently related to their tendency to be extroverted and outspoken. Due to how powerful they may be, a number three who cannot validate themselves and surrounds themselves with like extroverted or tolerant individuals may start to feel as though they must reduce themselves, which can result in destruction, either of oneself or others. A person who has chosen the three-destiny route will need to learn how to validate themselves and find allies who value and respect their creativity as well as those who can handle their louder voices and higher energy. Additionally, they will need to develop the ability to politely and discreetly distance themselves from anyone who does not accept them for who they are, since a loud argument will ultimately leave them feeling foolish and rejected.

Understanding that not everything goes their way is a significant life lesson.

The world has a structure that it flows with, despite the desire to be a free-flowing and adventurous person. As such, learning to flow with the world as it is will be a very significant life lesson. Threes often wonder why we even need work or why living expenses are so high, especially when it interferes with their ability to pursue their desired career path. They will gain a valuable lesson about how to fit in without losing a feeling of who they are by figuring out how to adhere to society without sacrificing their sense of independence and authenticity. A three will feel better in the long run if they can blend modern living with being unconventional or unusual.

CHAPTER 9

The Devoted Worker, Number 4

The energy of the number four is renowned for being one that centers on work and advancement. Fours are highly committed, organized, and practical. They are renowned for their propensity for putting in a lot of effort and their ambition to achieve a lot in their lifetime. They are motivated by a desire to advance in their lives and accomplish more.

Let's delve into the additional characteristics of the energy of number four.

Fourth Vibration

A number four vibrates with masculine energy since it desires to work and advance to put things in order. Despite being masculine energy, the number four is often tenacious energy that loves to see things through to completion rather than loud energy. They are the ones who will stay on the job until it is finished rather than clock out early because they enjoy feeling accomplished. Even if they enjoy praise and affirmation, a four energy will finish the task regardless of the praise they receive because their sense of success is sufficient. Words like dedication, constructiveness, practicality, determination, production, tradition, honesty, and pragmatism tend to connect with the energy of the number four.

The Psychic Number Four

The psychic number four manifests in people who are occasionally identifiable as workaholics. They tend to value their work and development above all else, and they struggle to find the motivation to remain dedicated to anything if they cannot see how it can be transformed into a goal that can be attained. They have a reputation for turning everything into a project, and once they have, they will come prepared with all of their energy, and they will do almost anything to achieve the desired outcomes.

A person with a psychic number of four will develop goals with varying time frames so that they constantly have something to strive for and may always have a sense of accomplishment. A four will feel more at peace with their existence the more they believe they are fulfilling their goals. A number four has to set daily and weekly objectives to feel like they are moving in the right direction, but at the end of the day, they are mostly focused on their larger goals, which are the ones that mean the most to them. They have objectives for every aspect of their lives, and they frequently have extremely specific ideas about what they want and how they want their lives to be. Fours frequently exhibit flexibility in their shorter-term aims because of their dedication to their long-term objectives.

They understand that this flexibility will enable them to achieve their longer-term objectives. Despite being flexible with their short-term objectives, the four are infrequently flexible about their long-term objectives. They want exactly what they want and won't accept anything less, so they'll fully ignore anything and everyone who might try to veer them off course.

The person who is number four is aware of what they want in life and also understands that they are the only ones who can make it happen. As a result, they put a lot of trust in themselves, and when that trust is betrayed for any reason, they get quite frustrated and nervous. A four feels completely out of place when they find themselves emotionally dependant on another person, depending on others to carry out a plan or make something happen, or in the exceedingly unusual case that they find themselves relying on others to assist them to complete a plan or make something happen. For number four, this feeling is terrible since it implies that they may never achieve their ambitions, which are still the most important things in their lives.

Fours are highly committed to being realistic and appreciating life as it is in addition to their energy and passion. They have an easy time embracing truth since they are realistic, regardless of how reality may appear to them. They adore having fun and taking part in activities that allow them to develop their abilities or challenge their minds, especially if these activities have a distinct objective or result. In other words, a four will gladly accompany a loved one to a movie night if they know they want to go. However, a four is more likely to prefer a round of golf or a night of bowling than a movie night.

A name number four

As people with a number four here want to transform their relationships into something with clear goals, four energy in the name number position can be complex and interesting. The four energy in this situation is already clear on what they want in a relationship and is probably already picturing themselves in any relationship, whether it be a friendship or a loved one. They will therefore probably have expectations, which can have both positive and negative effects on relationships. On the one hand, establishing expectations before entering a relationship allows you to steer clear of situations where you might be mistreated or incompatible with the other person.

The four energy, on the other hand, can be extremely possessive of their expectations, which could lead to you repeatedly ending friendships or relationships that don't live up to your obscenely high and possibly unreasonable standards. Despite your best intentions, you can discover that you don't allow for errors or realities in your interactions. However, when it comes to the relationship itself, you may be highly turned off by people who consistently fall short of your high expectations. In your mind, you are okay with people being real and raw.

In healthy relationships, you figure out how to have reasonable expectations and establish constructive relationship goals. Making your loved ones laugh frequently, letting them know they are supported and appreciated, and demonstrating your concern are all ways to feel accomplished. Instead of having just one objective, you set multiple goals that you can accomplish throughout time so that you always have something to strive for. This keeps you feeling motivated and optimistic about your relationship. Once you've established these objectives, you are very practical and realistic in your relationships, which makes you simple to get along with. Because you provide a space where they feel safe to work on who they are and develop themselves in your presence, people feel very peaceful around you.

You might turn into a destructive force in unhealthy partnerships. You have a propensity to try to change people or do their work, which makes you irritated when they are unresponsive.
When they remain the same, you either grow frustrated or realize that your efforts are not paying off as you had hoped, leaving you with a sense of unfinished business. You end up experiencing complete rejection in both of these situations, which makes you feel completely let down by your relationships. It's also possible that you may strive to make your connection happen regardless of what the other person wants because you have such a strong desire for it.
This may manifest as expecting someone to be your best friend even though they don't want to, or as wanting someone to be your wife or

husband even though they have made it apparent they are not ready or willing to wed you.

You can try to compel others to conform to the person you want them to be rather than respecting their wishes and accepting them. People may occasionally feel like you are treating them like a charity case or that they will never be able to please you since you are constantly trying to alter them.

Four as a Number of Destiny
You are reaching a stage of soul maturity if your destiny number is four. Your main goal in life is personal development since during this stage of life you will be working to apply life's lessons and advance as a person. A person on a four destiny route will frequently discover that they are drawn to a particular vision, which is frequently connected to their karmic journey or to what they have come to integrate during this lifetime.

Some people who choose one of the four routes may discover that their life lessons are more intimate than what a job can provide, and they may feel compelled to change careers occasionally when they achieve their goals and progress to learning the next bit of knowledge. They might work as a secretary, for instance, to develop their service skills, and then as a carpenter, to develop their investment in physical labor. In contrast, a person on a four-life route can have a single life goal, and everything they do will help them achieve it. This work is frequently extremely solid and predictable, but the specifics are always changing to keep the four destiny paths interested.

As an illustration, consider woodworking, where the four destiny paths might create different projects each time but the equipment and overall framework of the profession paths remain the same.

The four are focusing on two very distinct life lessons at the moment: integrating their karmic lessons and developing their spirituality.

The number four may be drawn to logic and reasoning at first in their life path, but as time goes on, they will start to embrace the incomprehensible and get intrigued by it. They will probably want to investigate it in depth.

To preserve the stability and anchor to the reality that the four destiny route seeks, it may be preferable for them to steer clear of any spiritual development that makes their reality seem distorted or incorrect. That is to say, while more extreme spiritual practices like astral projection and time travel may initially seem intriguing, they are ultimately far too unstable for the four destiny paths. Having said that, the four destiny route will find exciting and interesting topics such as comprehending meditation and the link to the divine or intuitive connection.

To better grow their spirituality and feel connected to their mission, they will want to put in the effort to forge that connection and start experiencing intimacy.

The four paths also have to improve its ability to let go of things, which is a crucial life lesson. The four destiny paths get very tied to what they want out of life and what they anticipate receiving, and when they realize that what they desire and what they are receiving is not the same, they feel very let down. Once more, the propensity to try and force others to change or situations to become what one wants can occur, which can result in toxic behaviors such as self-sabotage and occasionally manipulation of other people.

For a number four destiny path, it will be essential to learn how to separate from desired outcomes so that they can still find enjoyment in life generally, whether or not it looks the way they expected it to.

CHAPTER 10

The Adventurer is number five.

The spirit of number five is incredibly liberated, jovial, and adventurous. The energy of the number five values detachment, going with the flow and taking in everything that life has to offer. Five energies might be compared to a nomad that enjoys nothing more than tossing around and traveling wherever life leads them. Let's explore the number five energy further to understand what it is and how it impacts chart readings.

The fifth vibration

The feminine, freedom-seeking spirit of number five. You can get a good idea of what the five energy looks like by picturing a goddess dancing across a field of flowers, her hair flowing in the wind, and her arms reaching out to brush through the daisies. The five is someone who enjoys experiencing life and has reached a stage in their soul journey where they can do so with greater openness. The number five energy has a better knowledge of what life is and why it is here because it is more than halfway through its life cycle stages at this point. The deeper awareness is present within the five energy person's spirituality and emerges in their self-expression, even if they may not fully comprehend this information.

The Psychic Number Five

If your psychic number is 5, you probably have a serious travel blog obsession, are constantly adding travel-related pins to your Pinterest board, and want to get as many new stamps in your passport as you can. Fives are passionate about venturing out into the world and enjoying every variety of experiences there is to have. They love adventure and living life to the fullest. An individual with a five psychic number is the ideal travel partner because they are frequently ready for any adventure, are excellent resourceful thinkers, and know how to surrender to the experience and allow it to be as joyful as possible. A five may have a travel schedule for the things they want to do, but this schedule is frequently simply a guide so they can be sure there will be plenty of adventure during their travels.

The five will typically be open to making changes to their schedule as long as they get to enjoy all of the thrilling activities they had hoped to.
This kind of flexible planning is common not only in business trips but also in a five's regular day-to-day activities. If your psychic number is five, you probably prefer turning everything into an experience to make each day as memorable as possible. You might discover that others are always inviting you to join them on their travels, and you are usually more than delighted to accept.

You might meet a fascinating traveler who wants to take you out to dinner so you can continue the conversation by simply heading into your favorite corner store. You draw this energy into your life and everything becomes an adventure.
You are highly motivated by pleasure, and you frequently make decisions about your life based on what makes you feel good. Some may accuse you of living a reckless life since you find it difficult to settle down or lead a conventional lifestyle because it simply doesn't stimulate you enough. Everything you encounter is merely an experience.

You constantly strive to make everything as enjoyable as you can, from the people you associate with to the work you do. You are probably drawn to making everything as enjoyable as possible, such as by selecting a professional path that is more fascinating than a desk clerk or a banker, such as becoming a tour guide or a tree planter. The more thrilling and adventurous each area of your life is, the better in your eyes. Traditional ways of living are off-limits. You are the type of person that always has something to say, in addition to your free-flowing, pleasure-seeking habits.

You enjoy reliving your adventures, recalling them, and talking to others about them. Speaking about it gives you the feeling of reliving the experience, which can often be just as enjoyable as embarking on a thrilling journey. Additionally, by encouraging others to share their stories, you not only feel as though you are living vicariously through them but are also motivated to plan your next vacation. You probably have a strong interest in alternative and natural therapies for health and healing, which is another aspect of this liberating reality. When you have an upset stomach, you are significantly more likely to drink peppermint tea than to take an antacid. You might even be idealistic at times about how life should be, how health and healing should appear, and that all features of a typical existence should be abandoned in favor of a completely free and natural way of living.

The number five as a name
You are the kind of person who enjoys open-ended relationships if your name number position is five. You may discover it's difficult for you to genuinely settle into permanent relationships because individuals are continually entering and leaving your life.
Even though you probably have a limited group of close friends, chances are that your travels frequently keep you apart from them, thus your friendships are typically maintained more frequently online or over the phone than in person.

You probably run into these people whenever you are in town, but since you are not a homebody, likely, you don't mind if there is some distance between you and them. The only kind of friend you can maintain for a long time is willing to go on adventures with you and travel with you, but even then you are sure to drift away eventually. Although maintaining a close relationship in your life can be difficult, you will undoubtedly make every effort to find the appropriate partner for marriage.

When it comes to love, you long for a partner who can provide you with the excitement and pleasure you seek in a union. You enjoy the combination of adventure and pleasure, whether it is visiting a new restaurant to check out a dish you have never tried before or traveling to a new location to play about between the sheets. However, it can be difficult for you to settle down until you meet a partner who can combine pleasure with adventure. Your romantic relationship will probably be full of sensuality, comprehension, personal development, surrender, companionship, variety, and experiences if it is healthy. You benefit greatly from this kind of friendship, and as a result, you feel empowered to actively participate. If you are in a relationship that is bad for you, you can notice that you grow distant from the other person and find it difficult to be present in their company.

Even so, you might try to hang on if you feel that your life is lacking in pleasure since this starts to seem like a location where you can at least obtain something. In other words, because of how laid-back you can be at times, you tend to settle.
There's a potential that you and all of your buddies in a friendship will look very different from one another. Being so wildly different from one another makes you all somewhat similar. People with interesting lives and complicated personalities tend to be the ones

you spend more time with since they give you something to explore and comprehend. You enjoy attempting to understand others or, even better, failing to understand them since they are so unlike you. Being surrounded by such diversity keeps you interested in and fascinated by others around you, which fills you up socially.

Due to your love of freedom, you might discover that you regularly move on from relationships in both love and friendship. There are some persons with whom you may not communicate for weeks or even months before speaking with them once more as if no time has passed. Others will come and go, and while you will treasure the memories, other than the occasional Facebook or Instagram, you won't see them again.

However, it's likely that the majority of the people in your life greatly inspire you and are admired for all that they have contributed to your life. Every individual you've interacted with has been valuable to you in some manner, whether it was through the stories they shared, the advice they offered, or the inspiration they provided based on who they were. Everyone else seems to vanish into thin air.

Five as a number of Destiny
Your life's work will be to learn how to live a detached life and perhaps encourage others to do the same along the road if your destiny number is 5. Because of their inherent detachment, people with five destiny numbers frequently disseminate wisdom, even though they may not always fully comprehend it and apply it to their own lives. (In the seventh life path, wisdom is realized later.)

A five destiny number is frequently renowned for having lofty ideals about the future of the globe and being overly optimistic about its possibility. They think that if everyone adopted the same ideas, the world might instantly begin to mend, and they frequently secretly harbor the hope that this will occur throughout their lifetimes. They will continue to harbor the hope that this will come true in their lifetime even though they are pragmatic enough to recognize that it is unlikely. They want it so badly that they frequently surround themselves with individuals who are willing to conform to their vision, making it appear as though it is occurring at least in their world.

Others may be inspired to think that we can all calm down, take it easy, and just try to get along by this purpose of vision and idealism. The five destiny route instructs followers that it's OK to accept individuals for who they are and to distance ourselves from those who don't fit our worldviews. Accepting that we can have what we want and then continuing to work toward it every day can be the simplest approach to achieving it.

No matter how effectively the person on the number five destiny path shapes their reality, an entirely different reality that is absolutely at odds with what they have constructed still exists. To realize their idealistic life goal, people with the number five life path are occasionally careless and willing to disobey the law and do as they like. This can cause a lot of problems in life. Because they have not respected the fact that the general reality is very different from what they desire, some people may find themselves in disputes with other people or even the government. Given that the number five life path is frequently the exact opposite of the number four life path, commitment will be another important lesson to learn.

The number five is frequently distanced to the point of being faultless, in contrast to the number four's tendency to be attached and clingy.

For the number five to learn about commitment and consistency in life, it will be required to understand how to detach without entirely separating. Without this, the number five might find it difficult to commit, resort to adultery, be dishonest to preserve their freedom, or treat others unfairly or disrespectfully in favor of their enjoyment.

CHAPTER 11

The Harmonious Caregiver, Number 6

The spiritual development of the number six is starting to advance at this lovely number. You vibrate with the energy of the peaceful caregiver when you have number six energy in your chart. The harmonic caregiver is someone who values harmony and balance and who also has a propensity to desire to take care of and nurture others around them. However, this shouldn't be misconstrued for codependency or over-giving because a balanced, harmonic caregiver is naturally loving without going above and beyond what they might reasonably expect to receive in return.

Vibration at Number six

The frequency of the number six is similar to that of a healthy, balanced mother—or the idealistic mother that no one ever completely becomes. This is the mother who bakes cookies, maintains a nice appearance every day, completes her tasks, pays her bills on time, lavishes her children with love, and still has the stamina to be upbeat and optimistic at the end day. The harmonic caregiver vibrates at energy similar to that. The harmonic caregiver can do a lot and feel gratified by the act of giving, even though it is unlikely that they will be able to do it all without being exhausted. They enjoy giving and receiving thanks for their generosity because it makes them feel tremendously loved and valued by those they care about.

The Psychic Number Six

People may frequently refer to you as the "parent" of the group if your psychic number is six. You are probably the kind of person who is aware of everything going on in the lives of all of their loved ones, and you will gladly make time in your schedule to assist in any way you can. You can see that other people need your care, so you not only give your time when it is needed, but you can also anticipate the need and offer your assistance before anyone even asks. One of your most frequently asked inquiries is probably "how are you?" and once they have told you that they feel safe with you, they appear to open up completely to you. Even strangers will probably open up to you about their lives since they feel comfortable doing so. They can tell that you naturally take care of others and that you are a trustworthy person to share things with.

In your balanced state, you know exactly how to love unconditionally without hurting yourself.

You are an unconditional lover through and through. You understand when to keep individuals near to you in your circle and when to love them unconditionally from a distance. Because you are aware that everyone has good intentions and that every scenario was created with good purposes, you can let go of individuals and circumstances that are not right for you without retaining any negative emotions or anger. You understand that while some people may not always be able to act in a kind and considerate way, they rarely mean any harm.

In addition to how you care for and show up for people, you are also the type of person that is truly into being of service. You've probably done a lot of volunteering, either in the traditional sense where you signed up as a volunteer and donated your services or in more creative ways. This could take the form of anything from offering to hold the door open to bringing a homeless person out to lunch so you can feed them. It's likely that you have done both and that you do both frequently.

Sixes are renowned for providing stability and security when people need it, so they are not just about providing service in a more feminine manner. A six is not hesitant to provide you with a haven and shield you from whatever you are facing or, if necessary, from yourself.

Since they are aware of how crucial this is to the human experience, they will always try their best to intervene and ensure that everyone feels secure and anchored. They believe that everyone should honestly feel happy in their lives.

When a six is not serving someone else, they are probably performing the same acts of service for themselves.

A six will gladly spend their free time practicing self-care so that they can experience fulfillment and protection as well, even though it may occasionally require convincing for them to understand that they deserve the same amount of care. They do this in recognition of the rewarding nature of service, the importance of experiencing both the giving and receiving sides of it, and the knowledge that doing so fills their cups so they can continue to serve others. Regardless of the recipient, caring permeates all aspects of a sixes' life in some manner.

Six as a Name Number

If your name has the number six, you are probably the primary caregiver for your friends and loved ones. You are extremely passionate about taking care of the people you love, and you will constantly go above and beyond to make them feel loved and cared for. You are probably the kind of friend who offers to take a friend out when you know they have had a particularly difficult day, brings them gifts, and sends them "thinking of you" messages. You enjoy giving your friends both emotional and practical assistance, whether it be by listening to their grievances or by lending a hand when they need it to move or get their kids to school on time.

When you're in love, you like partnerships in which you can look after the other person, and you probably also like to be looked after. You probably have an image of yourself and your spouse caring for each other in your special ways in your perfect relationship dynamic. You may wish to assign certain caregiving responsibilities to each partner, such as you providing meals for the two of you and your partner clean up after them. Since you tend to be very altruistic in relationships, it is best for you to date someone who shares that trait, or at the very least, accept your tendency to be selfless and don't put unreasonable demands on you. If you don't learn how to set boundaries, your selflessness may in some situations cause you problems.

Sadly, some people might take advantage of your selflessness by being unreasonable in their demands or by frequently taking from you, which could lead to a relationship where you feel cheated and ignored. This unhealthy dynamic can significantly impair your self-confidence and self-esteem since it paints one of your most distinctive and cherished qualities as a flaw. Avoiding relationships with people who cannot be compassionate toward you in return is excellent to ensure that you may experience a harmonious relationship with your partner.

You can frequently be seen as the one in your friendship group who is most considerate. People tend to want to retain you in their lives for the long haul since they know they can depend on you in a variety of ways.

They like your willingness to always participate equally in relationships, your genuine concern for them, and your sincere compassion. Many people find your genuine concern for them to be inspiring and helpful in making them feel like they matter, which is a crucial characteristic in their eyes. A wonderful asset is being able to provide this to your friends. But just like in your relationships, you need to be careful not to surround yourself with friends who are excessively demanding or who don't appreciate the things you do for them. You run a high danger of being taken advantage of or underappreciated, and it hurts awfully when it happens.

To discover people that share your empathy and compassion, strive to maintain firm boundaries. Once you do, it will probably feel very rejuvenating for you because you will have made lifelong friends.

The Number Six as a Destiny

If your destiny number is six, you have a tremendous gift to give to the world and have come here with it. You are the exact opposite of the cruel and heartless people who populate our world today, which means that you have the qualities that this world desperately needs to see more of. Because it might not always be returned by others, your sensitivity and compassion might feel like a burden at times but know that the collective is healed by your very existence.

The individuals you interact with find great healing in your capacity to be sincere, to care about others, and impart your comfort and wisdom. You might discover that you're drawn to a line of work that enables you to care for others and spread this nurturing energy so that more people can benefit from it. You do your best to choose a job path that enables you to provide this energy to as many people as you can since you seem to intuitively know that just being in your care and compassion is healing. You are likely to choose a career that allows you to care for people, such as a daycare provider, therapist, nurse, retirement home care assistant, or something similar, especially if the people you are caring for are particularly susceptible to the dangers of the current state of society. Your life's lessons will probably center on understanding that not everyone is like you, developing healthy boundaries, and taking care of yourself.

You need to understand that not everyone will be as kind and sincere as you are, so you'll need to hone your intuition to make sure you're only putting your faith in really trustworthy individuals.

Recognize that not everyone is as kind as they could be, and take steps to keep yourself safe from those who choose to act unkindly toward you.

You run the risk of being a kind person who is taken advantage of if you allow bad people full access to your life by keeping them as friends or lovers. Setting limits will be crucial to ensuring that you are not taking on too much, even in your good connections. Despite how much you may like it, you shouldn't always be taking care of other people since there will be moments when you need to take care of yourself. By setting boundaries, you can make sure that you only keep friendships or relationships with people who can accept you for who you are and won't exploit you.

You must also realize that you deserve your care just as much as anyone else. To start taking better care of yourself, you must go past your propensity to prioritize the needs of others over your own. Admit when things are too much, be prepared to say no when necessary, and let go of the idea that you must cater to everyone's needs since it is untrue. To want or need to take care of yourself before taking care of yourself is not selfish, bad, or wrong.

In actuality, it is very typical. You will achieve a wonderful equilibrium that enables you to cultivate your impulses toward caregiving without putting yourself through mental or emotional hardship in the process if you are as kind to yourself as you are to others.

CHAPTER 12

The Truth-Seeker and Wise One (Number 7)

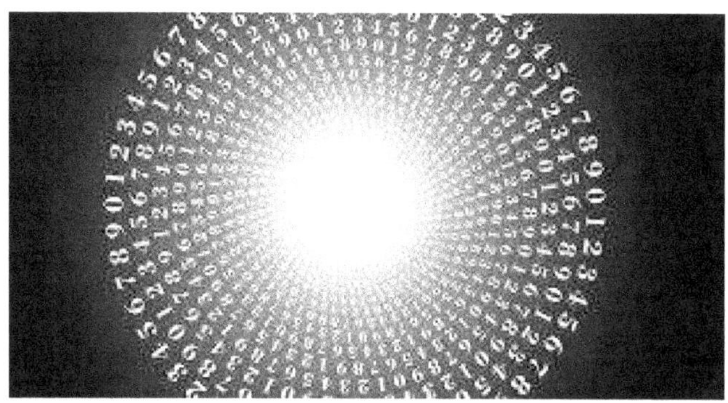

Seven is an extremely sociable and group-based number.
This number is frequently used to express the mood of the "collective" or of all people living on Earth at the time. This number is known to vibrate with energies of wisdom, knowledge, and truth. It is a very deep, contemplative number. Continue reading to find out more about what a seven in your chart represents.

Seventh vibration
Consider a knowledgeable elder with knowledge gained through life experience and introspection to obtain a clear idea of what a seven vibrates at. This elderly person has dedicated their entire life to learning about life, people, and how the universe appears to function. They are knowledgeable about everything, from love and human relationships to the sun rising and setting each day, and they are typically willing to freely impart this information to everyone interested in learning it. As if it were their gift, this elder appreciates the truth and will frequently see through anything that is not fundamentally true.

Even though this elder has a wealth of information, they freely admit that they do not know everything. As a result, they are always curious and willing to learn more from people around them. Everything necessary for the vibration of the number seven is present in this elder.

Wisdom, intense introspection, inner-selves, seclusion, philosophy, awareness, mysticism, emotions, knowledge, and discernment are words that usually ring true with a number seven energy.

The Psychic Number Seven

If your psychic number is seven, you probably consider yourself to be somewhat of a loner. As a result of how much you value your alone time and how eager you are to take on solo tasks, you may frequently be mistaken for an introvert. You are genuinely open to what alone has to offer, therefore you are not at all intimidated by dining alone, traveling alone, or living alone. However much you may like your alone time, you are unquestionably not antisocial or opposed to being around people. You probably like a reasonably healthy mix between being around other people and being alone because being around people offers you lots to think about later on when you are alone.

When a label places any kind of limitation on your life, you tend to avoid applying it to yourself. You realize how broad and lovely life is, and you think it is abhorrent to try to fit ourselves into small boxes with labels. You would much rather see yourself living freely and going from day to day without attempting to place any constraints on anything than trying to fit yourself into a box. This non-restrictive way of life provides you plenty of freedom to learn more about life, making you open to discovering new knowledge or different lifestyles that you might not have previously considered. In your opinion, the more easygoing and fluid your life is, the more you can remain open to the world around you, and that is your ultimate desire.

You desire to lead a truthful life and are unlikely to hide your thoughts or actual convictions. Due to your high level of discernment, you may choose to live following your truth rather than broadcasting it to everyone. You don't feel a strong desire to constantly update everyone on how your life is doing because you don't think it's necessary. It seems like a better use of your time to limit the information you offer to that which is pertinent or will help people.

As a result, you probably don't spend a lot of time on social media because you probably find it to be quite mindless. You would much rather be reading a fantastic book, having an intriguing conversation with someone who can teach you something, or teaching something to them.

You probably spend your time reading, studying, or writing down the information you learn. You enjoy calm reflection, so you might not comprehend why everyone in the current world seems to be always rushing around.

You think watching a movie or having dinner with friends is more fun than sitting still on your couch and gazing out the window.

In your quiet time, you think back on the information you've learned and put your views and understandings about the world around you together so that you can better understand life and people. You probably devote a lot of everyday time to this activity because you feel it is essential to your ability to make sense of the world around you. Without this time to yourself, you could feel agitated and overpowered by everyone around you, which might make you want to disappear for a bit. If you discover that those around you do not appreciate or acknowledge this, you may be inclined to withdraw inside yourself and become more introverted to avoid these people.

The name number seven
Your connections are likely highly deep and thoughtful if your name number is seven. You are likely surrounded by individuals who can either teach you something or whom you can teach something to, though it is more likely that one individual fulfills both of these criteria. You value friendships that focus on your personal development, and you enjoy witnessing your friends' personal development. You may meet people in settings like schools, study groups, museums, art galleries, or other locations that are rich in knowledge and history. As this is your favorite hangout space, you also frequently spend time there with friends or a romantic interest.

You probably have a really deep romantic relationship. You show consideration for the person you are in love with and invest time and effort in getting to know them and their interests. You enjoy getting to know your spouse completely because, in your opinion, it is one of the most intimate activities you can do together. You probably will be careful to make sure that the individuals you bring into your love life are genuinely willing to engage in this form of closeness because you feel like full knowingness and comprehension are a privilege. Hours of teaching each other, fact-checking together, and playing games that somehow involve trivia turn you on to an extreme degree. You appreciate developing and learning together, and you will be attracted to and feel the most affection for partners who respect these two aspects of your union as well.

Because you are more intellectual and analytical than you are emotional, you may find it difficult to express your emotions physically, which can sometimes make you seem cold or uninterested in a relationship. It may feel awkward to you to demonstrate love in other ways, like spending afternoons watching movies or having seemingly meaningless fun together, because to you, having healthy debates or attending study sessions together is the ideal way to do it.

You probably only have close relationships with a select few people in friendships. You value quality over quantity and would much rather spend your entire life getting to know a small number of people thoroughly than spend it only partially getting to know a large number of people.

However, you'll also probably find yourself conversing openly with other people who are quite knowledgeable once you have folks you're close to. You may make friends with a museum director and chat with them for hours about the exhibits and how they were made because you find this kind of interaction to be interesting. The individual may become your acquaintance or a passing ship in the night as you learn something about them and then go on, never to talk to them again, unless they truly feel deserving of your time and effort. Your close friends are very important to you, and you don't want to waste time hanging out with people. As these are the people who truly get you and who you truly get to, you tend to attract pals who are just as deep and introspective as you are.

That said, not everyone in your social circle is likely as knowledgeable as you are thus this may seem dull and repetitive. Instead, you are more likely to draw companions who are thoughtful, interested in complexity, and who generally have complicated personalities. By doing this, you can spend a lifetime getting to know them and enjoying and being interested in the very different ways in which they conduct themselves in life.

Seven as a Number of Destiny

If seven is your destiny number, you are dedicated to your goal of seeking the truth. Seven destiny numbers are drawn to any profession that satisfies their urge to continually learn more, therefore they frequently end up as yogis, professors, educators, tour guides, museum directors, historians, or any other occupation that fulfills this need. Your ideal job allows you to develop new skills and advance your career, in your opinion. To never get bored with the work you do, you want to master things but you also want to have a lot to master.

A person who educates the public about the truth as they perceive it may be drawn to you because you are likely passionate about truth-seeking in general. You enjoy informing people about corporate greed, the truth about where their food and clothing come from, and the most recent deeds of the government. You may also be informing others about fascinating facts or tidbits of knowledge just because you find them fascinating. You make it your job to stay informed and pass that information along because you believe it is your responsibility to ensure that the general public, or at the absolute least, your family and friends, are informed. You may sometimes be dubbed a conspiracy theorist or someone who is over because of how open you are to recognizing the truth behind things that many others simply ignore.

You're about to learn a big life lesson about when to share and when not to. While discernment is probably one of your strengths, you might discover that you often make decisions based on what feels right for you rather than what feels appropriate in the given circumstance. Because of this, you might open up and be honest when it is not optimal to do so and keep quiet when it would be better. Additionally, you are prone to pessimism and antisocial behavior, especially if you utilize your investigative abilities to go too far into notions about conspiracies and the like. You run the risk of adopting a jaded perspective of the world in general and coming to the conclusion that it's a bad place and that people are selfish and greedy. You have a great chance to remain objective and appreciate life for what it is by learning how to get over this jaded viewpoint rather than beating yourself up over every little thing. To educate yourself without depressing yourself, learn how to be open to discovering the facts without attaching too much personal emotion to it.

CHAPTER 13

The Strong Leader, Number 8

The number eight is a strong, influential number with a lot of superpowers. The number eight is a powerful one that is associated with abundance and success of all kinds. Eights are associated with material success, wealth, and freedom. Find out more about yourself if your chart shows an eight by clicking here!

Vibration at position 8

We have arrived at a stage of tremendous spiritual growth by the time we get to number eight in the numerological sequence. We've also arrived at the point where someone will want to start appreciating life for what it is now that they've made significant progress spiritually. Eights are self-assured, passionate about life, and eager to take full advantage of everything that the planet has to offer.

The vibration of eight has officially reached the point where they can learn how to enjoy these things tastefully since they understand that everything on Earth was created for us to experience. They have learned how to achieve success in a way that benefits everyone involved, hence they are typically not greedy or selfish nor will they do so at any cost. Having said that, the eight are also self-aware and blatant in their desire to savor life's finer things.

The Psychic Number Eight

You probably value influence, authority, and personal power if your psychic number is 8. You are a person who truly appreciates the finer things in life—someone who is in charge of themselves, who isn't hesitant to take charge in a situation, and who exudes a strong air of confidence. You consider yourself to be an "ancient soul" since you generally have good judgment and know things even when you don't know them. Since you often appear to know things that others are only now starting to grasp, the majority of knowledge to you is more about common sense than anything else. You can never be moved.

You have a strong desire for the world to be right, therefore you frequently use your leadership abilities and personal influence as a way to make decisions that benefit the group. You are sometimes referred to as a humanitarian since you genuinely want to see everything good with the world bloom while everything negative falls off. You will always make an effort to help peacefully. In whatever you accomplish in life, you are morally upright, conscientious, and extremely ambitious. You have a talent for seeing things clearly, which makes you exceptional at planning activities that involve big groups of people.

You naturally succeed at managing people and leading your team to success; it's almost as if you don't even have to try. You are well grounded in reality and realize that the world is your playground and that playing there is completely safe. You now have a thorough comprehension of life's workings and what it entails, enabling you to feel secure and at ease in almost any circumstance. But if you're not careful, you could start to have a superiority complex because you think you know more than other people and are more powerful than they are. As a result of trying to force others to follow your example, especially when they are not doing so voluntarily, can result in egotism and anger. You can try to press yourself on others and convince them that you know more, rather than respecting their freedom to say no.

Since the number eight resonates with the energy of karma, you might discover that this life cycle sees you fulfilling a lot of your karma. While it is painful and difficult, you may find that you now have all the information and abilities necessary to effectively neutralize this karma, making you appear to be capable of handling just about everything that comes your way. You eventually start to feel stronger with each obstacle you successfully overcome and see this as a strength in your overall leadership abilities.

Because of this, regardless of how difficult the lesson was, you usually look back on it as something you are glad you had the chance to learn in your lifetime. Nearly nothing feels too much for you to manage, and when it does, you can be highly resourceful and pragmatic about gaining the support you need to get through the obstacle. You can summon additional strength from your resources when you feel that you cannot complete a task on your own, provided that you have matured sufficiently to be willing to acknowledge your need for assistance and to approach others when necessary. This is why you tend to be so powerful.

The number eight as a name
If your name number is eight, your interpersonal skills are probably excellent. You certainly desire love and friendships that are visually appealing because you value connections that are all about flair and material possessions. You want to spend your time with individuals who dress as wonderfully as you do, attend the hottest clubs, dine at the best restaurants, and build your reputation by who you hang out with. Even though you probably get along with everyone, you choose to be around individuals who are concerned about their appearance and how they express themselves because they will represent you well since they represent themselves well. You desire to experience abundance, thoughtfulness, growth, and wisdom in

your interactions. Because you place so much importance on how things look and feel, you could occasionally be viewed as selfish in relationships.

You will probably choose partners in love who are more attractive than they are, which could be problematic. You tend to date attractive people who care about how you come across to others, which can occasionally put you in relationships with haughty people who aren't as great as they seem on paper.

However, your relationship is probably going to be the kind that people gush over on social media when you do find someone who is sincere and flashy like you. You will both dress nicely and keep your appearances up, both for yourselves and as a way to show respect to each other. Together, you govern the world thanks to your morality, your love of material things, and your broad awareness of what it is to live well. In addition to being strong motivators for each other to pursue their personal goals, you both tend to be very patient with one another. When two people join together in a healthy relationship, they become equally ambitious and protective of each other's dreams as they are of their own. Because you want you both to experience prosperity and abundance, you will exert every effort to further both your own and your partner's dreams.

me out as choosy when it comes to friendships since you genuinely don't want to hang out with people who don't care about how they look or how they appear to others. You find it very difficult to tolerate people who are untidy, slack, or disrespectful, and you won't likely keep them around for very long. You typically associate with the "elite" crowd, and you enjoy conversing with people who dress properly, care deeply about people, and speak and act in a manner that is respectful to others. You value appearance highly, therefore the better off your pals look, the better off you look. To feel confident that you are all supporting each other's development and ability to live a fulfilling life rather than holding one other back, you want to all come across positively.

You might find it difficult to build a social circle because of how much importance you place on physical appearances and how people present themselves unless you are ready to put yourself out there. Because their standards are too high for the average person and they are not always willing or able to fit in with crowds that seem to have higher standards, some eights find themselves in a constant state of loneliness.

Alternately, the person with the right name number can have encountered so many unfavorable arrogant people that they have grown cynical and find it difficult to believe anyone is as excellent as they claim to be. They may maintain a distance from everyone out of concern that they won't regret letting someone in.

Eight as A Destiny Number
If your destiny number is eight, you are probably here to demonstrate to others that there is nothing wrong with appreciating the finer things in life. You enjoy demonstrating to others how to dress opulently, enjoy riches, and openly welcome material possessions and wealth into their lives. You want everyone to see that they can have a wonderful life without it making them nasty people, therefore you live to disprove the notion that being affluent implies that you are naturally a selfish and rude person. There's a good chance that you'll choose a professional path that involves money, or anything that is in some manner opulent or wealthy. A banker, money coach or financial advisor, wealth advisor, manager of a high-end designer store, high-end designer, or even a luxury travel agent might be your

calling. In this lifetime, you are drawn to anything that has to do with wealth, luxury, and the finer things in life.

You're going to have to learn a lot of lessons, one of which is that not everyone is as fascinated by opulence as you are and that this is not necessarily a bad thing. It is crucial to learn to accept people for who they are and to be patient with those who are not as drawn to money as you are since there is no reason why everyone should be motivated by the same things as you are. Be cautious about your propensity to insert your ego into situations as this will seriously hinder you. Recognize when you are not on the same page as someone and accept it as a misalignment rather than labeling them as being beneath you or of a lower class. This is a valuable approach for you to worth and respect everyone without feeling forced to spend your time with people who do not feel like a good fit for you.

You should also watch out for your propensity to think that you know more than others or that your knowledge makes you superior to others. You may get into situations where you become narrow-minded or even like a dictator in your life because of how superior you may feel because you have reached a lifetime where you have a greater level of spiritual development.
It is effective to keep an open mind and to keep in mind that you are not the world's king. You might feel that way about yourself, but try not to let that degree of assurance make you believe that there is no more to learn and no room for life improvement. Always be eager to learn more than you already know and maintain your humility.

CHAPTER 14

The Humanitarian, Number 9

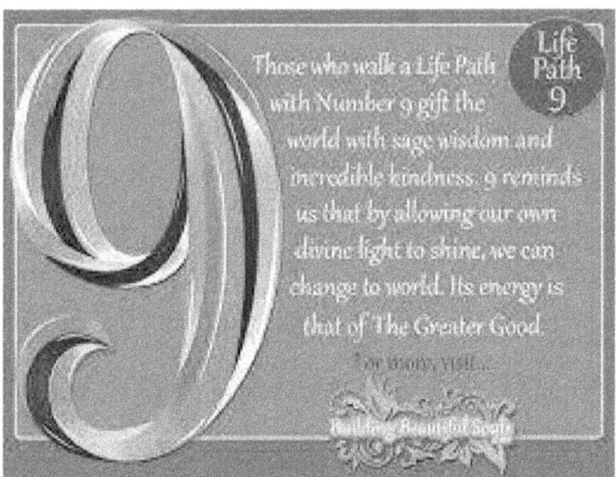

Nine is a symbol of spiritual maturity, service to others, and faith. The spiritual maturity of those who have a nine anyplace on their chart is high, or they have access to a high level of spiritual development. These people want self-acceptance, self-expression, empathy, freedom, and power. They have a propensity to be highly idealistic, and if they take the time to effectively develop themselves, they might wind up becoming the kind of person that many other people naturally look up to based on their very nature. Continue reading to find out more about what a nine in your chart means about you.

The vibration of the number nine

The vibration of maturity and sovereignty is associated with the number nine.

This is the last number in the single digits, which in numerology corresponds to the conclusion of a cycle. The fact that energy number nine is independent and powerful shows how smart this energy is. The people who often exist within number nine are the manifestation of the number nine energy. They practice wisdom rather than preaching it.

Rather than exuding confidence, they are confident. They are abundant rather than calling for abundance. Having a nine anywhere in your chart indicates that you are not only experiencing the things related to that area of your chart in your life, but you are also deeply embodied in them. Nine energy is very integrated and embodied. Having a nine in your chart indicates that you possess a level of maturity and sovereignty that the majority of people can only hope to have, which is a highly valuable quality that many people long for.

The Psychic Number Nine
If your psychic number is nine, you are probably a very poised person. Since most things in life just come quite effortlessly to you, you don't need to think too much about what to do or how to accomplish it. You possess exceptional intuition, sensitivity, empathy, and awakeness. You naturally have access to a higher level of mysticism and insight from the Divine than most people, yet this does not mean that you will engage in mystical or divinatory practices.

Even so, there's a strong chance you have a natural affinity for them and are tempted to give them a try on a gut level. You probably feel as though you already knew this information on some level when you learn about spirituality or Divinity, and it is only now being brought into your domain of awareness. Given that, you can become eager to allow even more knowledge to penetrate your field of awareness as you grow more curious to learn more.

You are probably quite drawn to being tapped into actions of humanitarianism as someone who has access to the highest embodiment of all.

You naturally exhibit philanthropy, generosity, and self-sacrifice since these traits are an integral part of who you are, so they don't feel forced upon you. You instinctively support the underdog, stand up for the weak, and give your shirt off your back to someone who needs it more than you do.

You could be surprised when others treat you like you are some sort of hero to others because these do not feel like heroic deeds. In your reality, this is just how things are supposed to be, and you are just carrying out your duties as a global citizen.

You have an extremely quirky personality, which makes people inquisitive about you. You often find yourself in the position of being a role model or an idol for them because you appear to them to exemplify the traits of the ideal person. Because you exhibit many of the qualities that are deemed to be good and because they wish to improve themselves, others may even consider you to be their mentor.

Your character has a high level of refinement and is inherent. Due to your very strong sense of self, those around you may get the impression that you are not normal and may even feel as though they know you well even though they do not. Because you can feel your sense of duty so profoundly in your bones, you rarely question who you are or what you are here to do. Regardless of the path, you choose in life, you experience it as an integral part of who you are rather than merely a means to an end. You have not only represented who and what you are, but you have also embodied the truth that the journey is at least as vital as the destination. Everyone around you can often detect your ancient soul qualities before you can, which makes you the epitome of the term.

As a Name Number, nine

Your relationships are probably based on service if your name number is nine. Even though you enjoy helping the people in your life, helping them jointly is something you enjoy even more. In other words, you are drawn to those who are equally charitable and giving as you are. You will exert all your efforts to surround yourself with people who share your admiration for their understanding of how their activities affect others and how they might help others so that everyone has access to a high quality of life. You are more likely to meet your friends and partners through volunteer work or charity events, where you are more likely to meet people who share your commitment to helping others.

You make the closest ties in love with those who will do anything to help others. Your ideal partner is probably someone who would gladly board a plane with you and travel to a third-world nation to support those who are struggling with the quality of life or to help construct a community. Your preferred dates involve attending posh charity galas or even getting dirty at a rally for animal rights. People that are enthusiastic, giving, and dedicated to their profession are attractive to you because you can relate to them on a deep level.

You are attracted to romantic deeds performed by persons who are kind, inventive, and genuine. A genuine person who is prepared to accept their imperfect reality is preferable to a person who makes an effort to appear better than they are. You probably fall into the category of people who are more impressed and flattered by what a present means to the recipient than by what it means to themselves. Even if you are not a huge reader, receiving a book from someone obsessed with books will feel like a big deal to you because you know how important that is to the person who gave it to you.

Additionally, you are appreciative of your partners who respect your independence, graciously exercise their freedom, and freely grant you your own. It is simpler for you to be true to the other person when you feel more confident that you can be yourself in a relationship.

You enjoy friendships with people who are willing to devote themselves to charity and service just as much as you do. You are motivated by people who share your interest, if not even more, and you probably spend a lot of time with your pals brainstorming charities you could start and talking about potential solutions to major global issues like starvation or animal abuse. You and your friends share a common passion to make the world a better place, and you live out this desire by making an effort to improve it every single day. People who have empathy, compassion, and responsibility appeal to you. Your buddies are probably a mix of eco-friendly vegans who are always teaching others about how to be better world citizens and how to help the world get better.

Your pals probably don't conform to societal conventions, steer clear of designer and name-brand goods because they're frequently associated with being terrible for the environment, and have a lot going on because they find it difficult to say "no" to assisting others. Although they are a diverse group of people, they all have the same fundamental desire for a secure and healthy environment for all Earth's inhabitants.

Nine as a Number of Destiny
Your life's work is probably centered on generosity, service to others, and humanitarianism if nine is your destiny number. If you do not operate a nonprofit organization, you probably work in a job that contributes in some way or at the highest paying position you

could find so that you can donate your own money to the causes you support. Your entire professional life revolves around supporting the causes that are most important to you, in one way or another. Your cause becomes your purpose in life if you discover that it is something that you are passionate about throughout your entire life, not just when it comes to working.

You are fervently committed to what you do and will give it as much of your time and resources as you can, whether you are working for animal welfare or better living circumstances in third-world nations.

You have a huge responsibility to complete any lessons you still need to learn in life. You have reached a stage in your spiritual development where you must be acutely aware of the teachings you have been learning to finish them. This will only enhance your embodiment and capacity to be the finest version of yourself, enabling you to interact with the world even more. Finishing these lessons will also provide you with a profound sense of closure, clarity, and calm, allowing you to begin fully and deeply enjoying your life. This does not imply that life will be simple for you or that there won't be any more lessons to learn or difficulties to overcome, but it does imply that you will start finding it simpler to face these difficulties from a more complete state of being.

Realizing that not everyone is as generous as you are and coming to terms with that will probably be a difficult lesson for you to learn to overcome in life. This can make you feel very negative and furious with the world in general. You can find yourself becoming irritated with those who do not support or understand your cause. When someone disagrees with you, you can feel so enraged or angry that you treat them cruelly or meanly, which would be unfair. You need to be careful to maintain your zeal without violating the rights of others or acting cruelly in support of your beliefs.

It's crucial to keep in mind the adage "you catch more flies with honey than with vinegar" in this situation.

CHAPTER 15

Master Numbers and Double-digit Numbers

When it comes to numerology, double digits, master numbers, or repeated double digits like 11, 22, and 33 can all be used to convey certain meanings. Even while we typically desire to combine multiple numbers into a single number, there are situations when reading a number whole or reading it along with its sum might help us understand it better. You will discover the meanings of double-digits and master numbers in this chapter, as well as how to interpret them in numerology readings. Additionally, you will learn when to combine multiple digits into a single number for reading and when to leave them alone.

Double-Digit Significance

In numerology, we rarely maintain a double-digit unless there is an exceptionally compelling reason to do so. Seeing a double-digit number everywhere is one situation when you might be receiving a special message from this combo. The energies connected with the numbers 4 and 2 together, for instance, may be highly pertinent to you at this point in your life if you are seeing the number "42" everywhere.

There is just one other instance in which a double-digit number will be significant, and that is when a double-digit number is reduced to a single digit unless you are seeing a double-digit number repeatedly like this. For instance, you can utilize the energy of 5 and 4 to better understand what this particular 9 energy will be like if you multiply 5 by 4 to reach 9. It's likely to be significantly different from the energy of a 9 produced by adding 1+8 or 3+6. The deeper energy concealed behind a single digit is what you are reading in this instance rather than merely a double-digit.

Here are a few different interpretations of 9 energy based on the aforementioned combinations to help you understand what I mean:
9 = 5+4: This particular nine energy is probably associated with effort and adventure, therefore the person is probably a humanitarian who wants to serve abroad and do physical labor. Instead of serving as the event's treasurer, this specific humanitarian is more likely to be spotted drilling wells for clean water or constructing shelters for the destitute.
9 = 1+8: Since this humanitarian is very strong and likely a leader, they are more likely to be a project manager. They will be the ones in charge of leading teams of nonprofit leaders or running their charity while keeping everyone else in line.

They are in charge of making schedules, organizing activities, maintaining order, and guiding the organization toward success in attaining its humanitarian objectives.
9 = 3 + 6: This compassionate person is more likely to manifest as a talented caregiver. They want to be the ones taking care of the young, the old, or anyone else who would benefit greatly from their innovative and expressive approaches. In doing so, individuals can look out for others and enjoyably express themselves, which eventually increases their capacity to give back.
As you can see, each of these nine energies is a humanitarian as you might think, but how they manifest as a humanitarian depends on the two-digit number that gave rise to their respective nine energies.

To better understand who you are and what you are producing in life, using double-digits in this way might help your chart gain more depth and clarity. Look at your alternative double-digit numbers to see if you can identify with them if you can't completely relate to what your primary number has told you. Having a better grasp of who you are and how to follow your core energy in a way that genuinely feels good for you may result from doing this.

Indicative Numbers

From 11 to 99, master numbers are repeating double-digit numerals. In the section below titled "Repeating Master Numbers," you can read more about the specific master number styles that are triple, quadruple, and higher digits believed to be.

According to legend, master numbers contain both the enhanced energy of the single-digit numbers to which they are connected and some of their unique meanings. If a master number appears in your reading, you should never reduce it to a single digit because it is regarded as a sacred number all by itself. Each master number's meaning is summarized below in case it appears in your reading.

11th Master Number: This master number is frequently thought of as the number of angels or the Divine and is thought to be associated with a high level of spiritual development. If you have a strong intuitive connection to master number 11, you are being divinely guided to the utmost degree possible. One of the purest numbers on the earth is this one.

Master Number 22: This number reflects innovation and design because it is linked to the number of master builders. If number 22 appears for you, you will have the power behind you to realize even your most ambitious life goals. In most cases, the master number 22 is only kept as a master number if it appears in your numerology chart. You should lower this number to a number four energy if it appears elsewhere.

Master Number 33: Master number 33 is revered in many different religions and is regarded as being the master teacher. The themes of this song are harmony, peace, and artistic expression. This number resonates with both the meanings of 3 and 6, hence its meaning reflects both.

Master Number 44: The master healer is represented when this master number appears, making it one of the more uncommon ones. This number is a strong one for healing because it has high vibrational energy when it comes to work and strength. Anyone with the number 44 in their chart is probably easy-going, witty, and highly grounded.

Master Number 55: People that have master number 55 in their chart tend to be very independent, tenacious, and adventure-seeking. A person with the astrological number 55 will probably choose to navigate life alone because 55 = 10 and 1 is the result. They may find it difficult to establish long-term relationships since they place such a high importance on their liberties.

Master Number 66: The transformational number is represented by the master number 66. People are bringing in a lot of transformation and potent knowledge at this energy. A person with a 66 on their chart is likely to have a strong desire for justice, be extremely compassionate, have a positive attitude toward life, and strive for perfection in everything they do. They are also prone to idealism.

Master Number 77: Intuition is a quality embodied by this master number. A 77 in their chart is perfectly positioned to communicate with higher realms of knowledge and serve as a sort of collective prophet. Due to their innate intuition, these people won't likely need

to put in a lot of effort to tune in to and follow their intuition. If they try to ignore their intuition in any manner, they
may feel quite out of place and find it easier to stay connected to and follow their intuition.

Master Number 88: Master Number 88 is a very powerful number to have in business, especially in a business that requires the use of masculine energy to be run effectively. A business that needs a strong leader will benefit from having one who is in tune with the energy of master number 88. This energy is analytical and effective, and it wants things done right and on schedule.

Master Number 99: The themes of embodiment, leadership, and wisdom are represented by this number. If the master number 99 resonates with you, you should use this as a message to embody your wisdom and leadership skills so that you may help others navigate life. You will feel more at peace in your life the more fully you embody these two attributes.

Using Master Numbers Again
You should interpret master numbers that appear repeatedly or that align with three or more of the same number as an indication that the energy associated with that master number has been greatly amplified. The more often a number appears in your environment, the stronger its energy is for you, and the more you must pay attention to and internalize its lessons. Two separate repetition patterns—having several digits in a single area or appearing for you again over some time—can indicate the presence of repeating master numbers.

If you notice numerous numbers in a single location, such as three consecutive sets of the master number 11 or the master number 11 appearing three times in a contract in important locations, you should be aware that the master number 11 energy is potent with that specific item. While the energy may not necessarily be present everywhere in your life, you should pay great attention to that area and concentrate on how you may incorporate the wisdom or energy of master number 11.

Most of the time, when you comply, you'll discover that things go much more smoothly for you than they would have if you had completely disregarded the warning.

If a number appears repeatedly over some time in numerous locations, it is a sign that you should incorporate this energy more fully into your everyday life. People frequently use the occurrence of the number 11:11 as an example of this. The number 11 may appear frequently in your daily life, pull you to look at the clock at 11:11 every day, or even appear at random, like on your supermarket bill or on your friend's new phone number. If a specific number appears to be following you, it means that you need to incorporate that energy more fully into your life.

PART 3
LIFE AND NUMBERS

CHAPTER 16

Numbers For

You can use numbers to align yourself with more of what you want in life in addition to using them to learn more about yourself. Numerology can be used to improve a variety of things, including your sense of balance and financial prosperity. A fun approach to attract more of what you desire and connect yourself with more of what makes you happy in life is to use numerology in these areas of your life. You will discover how to use numerology to improve your life in this chapter.

Counts for Cash

We all have a specific amount we need to make it in life. Since the number of money resonates with one, you can determine your money number by taking your psychic number, multiplying it by one, and then reducing it to a single digit. With the example birthday of September 14, 1957, you can see in the example below how to reach your money number.

Numbers for Birthdays Plus 09, 14, 1957, 1 in money Equation
$0+9+1+4+1+9+5+7+1 = 37, 3 + 7 = 1$
Amount in Money: 1
You can get a feel of how you typically relate to money once you have determined your money number. This number can also be used in your methods for manifesting money, such as by setting aside funds for things that have meaning for you in terms of your number. Saving \$1, \$10, \$100, etc. would be wonderful if your number was 1.
Based on your money number, here is a handy sheet for how you probably relate to money:

Money Number 1: You enjoy having control over your finances and getting paid fairly for your work.

Money Number 2: Your financial decisions are prudent.

Money Number 3: You are a skilled communicator and negotiator in financial matters.

Money Number 4: You choose traditional professional paths and put a lot of effort into earning money.

Money Number 5: You take pleasure in buying, selling, and negotiating with others.

Money Number 6: You must have a stable job.

Money Number 7. You enjoy earning money through technological employment

Money Number 8: No matter what, you'll always be good at making money.

Money Number 9: Your primary goal when earning money is to give it away.

Numbers to Inspire
The vowels in your name—a, e, I o, and u—are added together to form your motivation number by adding their respective numerological values. Here is a cheat sheet that will allow you to figure out what your motivation number signifies and an example of how to do it using the name

Sam Smith.
Person: Sam Smith
Wav: A I
In mathematics, $1 + 9 = 10$ and $1 + 0 = 1$.

Objectivity Number
1 You can find out what your motivation number is by using the alphabet cheat sheet from Chapter 4. Once you've located it, the numbers below will assist you to understand what your number indicates about your level of motivation in life.

Your first source of motivation is your desire for autonomy, accountability, and creativity.
You are inspired by working in groups, whether it is to start a family or collaborate with others to implement a company idea.

The third source of motivation is your need to interact with others, your desire to express yourself creatively, and your need to communicate.

You are inspired by custom, routine, and being a homebody, according to Motivation Number 4.

You are motivated by your desire for anything novel and unusual, and you perform best in environments free of routines and repetition.

Your family and your daily life at home are your sixth and seventh sources of motivation.
You enjoy looking after your family and maintaining order in the home.

You are driven by your ongoing curiosity and want to learn more and gain more knowledge, which is motivation number seven. You enjoy thinking about the cosmos and existence itself.

You are motivated by big projects, especially those that have to do with management and leadership. You are more interested in a project the bigger it is.

The ninth motivation is your desire to help others and mankind as a whole. You also like being able to give back.

Hidden Passions Numbers

Numerology can help you discover your hidden talents and passions because we all have them! Discover what you could be interested in or excellent at that you aren't yet aware of by using the equation below to obtain your hidden passion number! By keeping an eye out for patterns in your name's numerals, you can discover your secret passions. You should thus take your name, calculate the numerical value of each letter, and then pay particular attention to any repeated numbers. The value of this number reveals your hidden desires!

You can have many, as a hint!

To determine the ideal format for a hidden talent chart, we'll use the example name, Kevin Clark.

Call sign: Kevin Clark

K = 2, E = 5, V = 6, I = 9, N = 5, C = 3, L = 3, A = 1, R = 2, and K = 2 are the numerical values.

Numerals that Recur: 2 (3 times,) 5 (2 times,) 3 (2 times.)

Secret Desire Numbers: 2, 5, 3.

You can get a sense of what your secret passion numbers are once you have determined which numbers appear repeatedly in your name. Here is a handy sheet explaining what each number can indicate about your hidden passions.

First Hidden Passion: You are a leader and a warrior. You probably gain speed in competitive activities like politics or athletics.

Hidden Passion No. 2: You have a keen intuitive sense. You probably move more quickly when you're doing activities that call for perseverance and patience, like painting or model-making.

Your third hidden passion is that you love to party! In social and physically demanding activities like dance, comedy, and team sports, you probably accelerate.

4th Hidden Passion: You are methodical and well-organized.
No matter how big or little your goals are, or what industry they are in, you move faster toward achieving them.

You are an explorer and a traveler, which brings us to hidden passion number five. You are quick to adjust to change and probably have a great command of language. Working in public relations might be beneficial to you.

Hidden Passion Number 6: You are a dreamer and you love being of service. You become more active in helping your neighbors and loved ones. You'd be a fantastic companion, friend, or housekeeper, as well as a humanitarian.

Seven: You have a high level of intelligence and intuition. You progress quickly in your study and meditation practices, and you'd be an excellent spiritual mentor or instructor.

8th Hidden Passion: You are incredibly powerful and accomplished. You become more adept at leading others, inspiring others to perform better, and determining the strengths and limitations of others.

You are a warm, sympathetic, and giving person, according to Hidden Passion Number 9. Even if you may have had this talent concealed deep within you since you were a little child, you progress quickly in being a creative genius. This seems to be a trend among people with hidden passion number 9!

Compatible numbers

What numbers are you most compatible with if you want to know if you are a good fit for the person you are thinking about starting a friendship or romantic relationship with?
Numerology charts, like astrological charts, include compatibility information and can be compared to the charts of friends or partners to see how compatible you are. You will use your psychic number to gauge a person's compatibility.
The most compatible numbers are shown in the following table.

Quantities for Balance

Until you realize that your life is out of balance, your balance number won't often have an impact on you. This number can be used to help you figure out how to get through emotional upheaval when your life has become out of balance so that you can start recovering from the imbalance. Adding together the initials you were given at birth will give you your balance number. Your initials would be T, D, and S if your birth name was Toby David Smith. You may determine the numerical value of your balance number once you have determined the numerical value of your initials.

Here is an example equation that demonstrates how to arrive at this figure. To locate your balance number, see the alphabet table in Chapter 4.
Birth name: Toby David Smith
TDS, TDS, and S
Initials' Numerical Value: T = 2, D = 4, S = 1.
Formula: 2 + 4 + 1 Equals 7.
Balance: Seven

Once you've identified it, you may hang onto it and use it as a reference point whenever you notice an imbalance in your own life. The meaning of each balance number and how to use it to help you create balance in your life are explained below.

Balance No. 1: Continue to rely on your resources for strength, but learn to communicate with others in your personal and professional life.
Learning to break out of your natural independence and ask for help will be helpful when you need to find balance.

Balance Number 2: Because you are a highly emotional number, understanding how to transition from strong emotional reactions to more realistic and reasonable ones might be useful.
Consider your position carefully, then take the next logical action. Your feelings will appreciate it.

Balance No 3: Refrain from getting overly emotional or attempting to manipulate your way out of issues you encounter. Practice separating yourself from the issue so that you can view it more objectively. By doing so, you'll be able to see the issue for what it is and identify a workable solution to help you forward.

The fourth balance is to approach your problems with greater humor and to be aware of your feelings. In most circumstances, trying to push through and force your way forward would just result in more issues. It will be beneficial to learn how to be more tender and sympathetic.

Balance No. 5: Avoiding difficulties will only make them worse because you may find yourself doing it repeatedly. Find a way to center your free spirit while tuning into a sensible course of action. It can be beneficial to develop the ability to endure discomfort because it will help you get through your issues. They're frequently not as frightening as you imagine.

Balance No. 6: You have a strong capacity to comprehend the difficulties you are facing and to view them from various perspectives. You can perceive the opposing viewpoints, which aids in your quest to learn how to come up with a peaceful solution.
Just be sure to include your perspective in problem-solving so that you feel included, too.

Balance No. 7: Trying to isolate yourself won't help you right now. Although you might want to isolate yourself, this is not what you need. Spend time reflecting, but also be prepared to face your emotions, and then collaborate with others to find solutions to your difficulties. To prevent being overtaken by your emotions, maintain composure and ease when expressing your feelings.

Balance Number 8: Refrain from attempting to exert total control over and force your way through any situation.
Instead, softly access your emotions, and talk to your wants, and feelings. It is acceptable to take the initiative and lead the way, but make sure you do so with kindness and tenderness.

Balance Number 9: Ask people for advice and be sympathetic to their predicaments. A terrific opportunity to "feel" into the best answer for you is to sympathize with people who have experienced what you are going through since you relate easily to other people. This will enable you to have a more comprehensive perspective and solve problems effectively.

CHAPTER 17

Tarot, Astrology, and Numerology

Tarot, astrology, and numerology are all related. Each of the three 3 reading approaches has a distinctive way of fitting in with the other two, yet they all come together to create a potent reading format for everyone. You might be shocked to hear that numerology is not all that dissimilar from astrology or tarot if you have ever been inclined to either of these reading techniques. Continue reading to discover more about how they are all related.

Astrology and Numerology Relationship

According to astrology, which studies how the planets and stars move about one another, the meanings of the planets vary depending on where they are in the sky. There are twelve houses, or stations, in astrology that a person's chart will "pause in." Each of these houses is controlled by a different planet, and the meaning of the planet frequently corresponds to the meaning of the house's number.

A cheat sheet with the 12 various houses' astrological and numerological connotations is provided below.

Aries, the independent and tenacious leader of the zodiac, rules over House 1. Number 1 is also associated with self-reliance, fortitude, and leadership.

House 2 is ruled by Taurus, a stable, steadfast, and change-averse sign. Number 2 is equally detail-oriented and does not like abrupt changes.

Gemini, a friendly, intelligent, and quick-witted sign, rules over House 3. Additionally, number three is linked to sociability, competence, and fast thinking.

House 4 is ruled by the sensitive, maternal sign of Cancer, which is infamous for having erratic moods. The number four is noted for being steady and composed, albeit reactive, which means that their moods can change very quickly.

House 5: This sign, which is ruled by Leo, is brash, arrogant, and occasionally dramatic. They yearn to be free. The number 5 is a proud, pompous, and occasionally theatrical number that loves freedom.

House 6: Virgo, the sign that rules this house, is meticulous, anxious, and fastidious. They prefer things to be done in a particular way, which ties into point number 6.

House 7: Led by the sign of Libra, this sign is highly reflective, appreciates fairness and balance, and occasionally lacks clarity. The number seven is also recognized for being exceedingly reflective, thoughtful, and balanced.

House 8: Scorpio, the sign it rules, may be exceedingly tyrannical, passionate, and even vindictive. They enjoy having power.
Number 8 is also quite dominating, likes to be in charge, and occasionally feels extremely passionate to the point of seeking retribution.

House 9: Sagittarius rules this sign, which has a free-spirited, philosophic, and careless side. This is how number nines are as well, and they are greatly influenced by others.

House 10: Capricorn, who rules this sign, is highly practical and frequently aloof in their demeanor. They enjoy careers and public stature.

Number one is frequently quite chilly and realistic in their leadership style, and they also desire popularity, according to the breakdown at position 10.

House 11 is ruled by Aquarius, a sign that is friendly, outgoing, and frequently distant. This connects with the energy of master number 11, which is also deeply invested in these traits and is occasionally referred to as an Earth Angel.

House 12: Pisces is the ruling sign of this sign, which is sensitive, romantic, and reserved. The number 12 is renowned for being exceedingly sensitive, very emotional, and suspended between the material and spiritual realms.

Relationship of Numerology to Tarot

Tarot and numerology are closely related since each of the 78 cards in a normal deck of cards have a specific number attached to it. When reading tarot cards, it is important to consider the card's suit number because it affects the interpretation. For instance, a card with the number one on it will signify a fresh start in that specific area of life.

The following is a fantastic cheat sheet that explains how numbers apply to tarot readings:

Number 1: Denotes fresh starts and the outset of a journey. This is frequently regarded as the most basic component of each suit in the tarot and typically emerges when a person is about to embark on a new endeavor.

Number 2: This is the partnership number, and it frequently represents the decisions a person will make in life. Any suit's number two card will frequently appear during a period of reflection or introspection and assist a person in choosing the course that their life should be following.

Number 3: In the tarot, the number three represents a situation's growth and natural progression. This is the point where an idea develops into a brand-new method, propelled by the vigor of number three. This is the social and team-building number.

In the tarot, the number four stands for foundations. We are vibrating at the energy of pragmatism and organized thought in this number. When a particular level of success has been attained and the person is prepared to build on that achievement, this card will come.

Number 5: If a card bearing the number five appears in a reader's reading, instability and change may enter that person's life. Any fives in a tarot deck frequently exhibit this instability as well, which is consistent with the number five's energy, which is one of freedom-seeking and adventure.

Number 6: When you pull out a card with the number six, you are stepping out of the flimsiness of the energy represented by the number five.
The number six card frequently depicts a sense of community, which inspires people to connect with those in their support network in some way.

In a tarot reading, the number seven signifies a request for you to have confidence and patience while you travel. You will probably go through a time of self-awareness and contemplation at this point to complete whatever growth phase you are presently working on.

Number 8: The number eight in the tarot deck represents advancement.
You may be sure that you have been achieving a high level of success in some aspect of your life when the number eight card appears. Currently, you are handling things effectively there and receiving praise for a job well done.

Number 9: Just as it would in numerology, the number nine in tarot represents the end of a cycle. Even though the tarot deck only goes up to number 10, it is at number 9 that this completion cycle first manifests.

Number 10: This is the last card in the sequence and, according to the numerology and tarot link, it denotes the precise moment before we move from completion to a fresh beginning once more. This is the period just before a new life begins.

CHAPTER 18

9-Year Cycles

According to numerology, everything is a cycle. 9 cycles to be precise.

Numerology holds that everything is a cycle, from the single digit of number 1 to the single digit of number 9. This indicates that a new cycle is completed at ages 9, 18, 27, 36, 45, 54, 63, 72, 81, 90, and 99. You may assess where you are in life and what you are currently working on generating or manifesting by knowing where you fall within a 9-year cycle.

You can see what to anticipate for each annual cycle in the table below.

1st-year cycle

It's possible to connect your year-one cycle to new beginnings and fresh starts.

This is where you sow the seeds for the knowledge and growth you will acquire over the next nine years. Here, pay great attention to what you are starting since it will help you learn the lessons you need to learn in the future.

2nd-year cycle

Year two is a year of slow advancement. Avoid placing too much pressure on yourself to finish everything or go on to the next step since you don't want to move too rapidly. Instead, concentrate on expanding your network and making connections with people who will be able to support you in the future. Keep these connections strong.

3rd-year cycle

You should concentrate on building happiness throughout the next three years. You may have given people more of your attention during the past two years as you cultivated your relationships for your future development. Put more effort into serving and bringing in your happiness this year. You have the opportunity to grow even more and put your development into action here.

4th-year cycle

Four years is meant for significant progress and transformation. You will notice that your efforts are producing a lot of fresh successes in the fourth year of any cycle. Although it is clear that you have not yet achieved your goals, this year will present you with numerous chances to demonstrate your development.

5th-year cycle

You'll have more new experiences in year five, especially ones that are important for your development. You will have many opportunities throughout a year five cycle to learn through exploration, travel, and change. As this will be a highly hands-on year for you to embrace your growth, you will also learn from your missteps.

6th Year Cycle

After a year of development and transformation, the sixth year is your chance to remake yourself. This is where you will begin to take a closer look at your journey and make decisions about what feels right for you and what you want to achieve in your life. Your connections will be cultivated as you find balance, healing, and greater love.

7th-year cycle

The seventh year of your cycle is the one for personal growth and exploration.

Here, you'll examine all of your personal development from the inside out and explore ways to accept and live it. You will begin to notice changes in the lessons you have been working through over the previous seven years as you start to completely comprehend what they all represent, frequently in retrospect.

8th-year cycle

A year eight cycle is all about gaining personal strength and self-assurance. You are progressing further this year into a state of self-awareness and self-development. As you grow more assured in your knowledge and your ability to apply it to your life, you are beginning to reap the benefits of your teachings. You'll accomplish a great deal this year.

9th-year cycle

You'll discover that you're doing a lot of reflecting in year nine. You will be reflecting on the past nine years to see what you have achieved and learned throughout this time.

Think of this as a time of consolidation in your life when you come to understand what everything meant, how you have changed as a result, and what you can formally let go of.

CHAPTER 19

Reincarnation and Numerology

The nine separate cycles are thought to have connotations about each incarnation in addition to ones belonging to each year. According to numerology, you will reincarnate nine times, with each time being guided by teachings related to the number of previous incarnations. You will learn what is supposedly meant by each incarnation in this chapter. Based on what your destiny number is on your numerology chart, you can determine what incarnation you are currently in.

first manifestation

As you are in your first life cycle, it is stated that your initial incarnation on Earth was relatively innocent. Your spiritual development is still in its infancy for this life cycle, and you haven't had a lot of chances to learn about Earth itself. Your soul is not young since this is your first physical manifestation, but it is fresh to Earth.

Secondly Manifested

Connection and stability are key themes in your second life. You'll probably make connections with your soul family in this lifetime, or with other spirits who came to Earth specifically to meet you and work through your karmic lessons. As you move away from the ferocious independence of your first life cycle, you will spend this lifetime learning how to respect and value the connections of others.

Threefold Incarnation

You are probably going to be more extroverted and interested in Earthly pursuits in your third life cycle since your soul is beginning to recall what life is all about. Being that you haven't yet figured out how to fully enjoy life with other people, this will have a highly immature or self-centered perspective. While other individuals will undoubtedly be present, you are more likely to regard them as a part of your experience than as a part of the experience that you are all having together.

Fourth incarnation

Performing soul work will be the focus of your fourth existence. You will start to mature more at this point, and with that maturity may come some suffering or pessimism. The truth of nonduality, or of being autonomous in a vastly interconnected collective, is beginning to dawn on you. So to speak, you'll be doing a lot of soul-searching.

Incarnation No. 5

When you start enjoying freedom and adventure in your fifth incarnation, it will be a big departure from your serious and concentrated fourth incarnation. You will spend your entire life resisting your natural tendencies to learn new things about the world. In this stage of your life, you want to see, study, and experience as much as you can.

Sixth incarnation

You're going to start settling down during your sixth rebirth. Your soul will be seeking to learn the experience of settling down and embracing commitment after an incarnation of adventure and independence. You will get knowledge on how to effectively commit to living as a member of a community or a group.

Incarnation No. 7

You'll probably spend most of your life cycle studying because your seventh incarnation is all about growth and learning.

You are beginning to bring all you have learned throughout the prior six incarnations together, and you are doing this through the reflective and inquisitive seventh incarnation.

8th Incarnation

In your eighth incarnation, you are building on the knowledge you acquired in your seventh one so that you can start embodying the real power of your soul. To ensure that your new knowledge is experienced on some level, you'll probably want to micromanage how it is integrated into your current life cycle.

Incarnation No. 9

You are thought to be in your ninth incarnation—your final life cycle—and will experience true embodiment during this cycle. In the past nine life cycles, you have encountered numerous dualities and lessons, and at this point, you are embodying them on a soul level with a deep soulful maturity. Throughout this life cycle, you are displaying who you are.

CONCLUSION

Having finished Numerology for Beginners, congratulations!

This book was created to assist you in exploring the enormous field of numerology and starting to grasp the potential of this divination instrument. Numerology is a highly useful tool that has been around for a while and can help you learn more about yourself and how to live your life following who you are. You can explore the vast world of you from a completely new angle by tuning into your numbers and learning how to read your chart.

I sincerely hope that this book has helped you gain a better understanding of numerology, including what it is, why it is significant, how it functions, and its practical applications. Learning how to make and interpret your chart and using it to apply numerology to your life can be effective. Through this book, I hope you were able to gain a deeper understanding of who you are, connect with your numbers, and experience a stronger sense of self-consciousness and personal awareness.

After reading this book, the next step is realizing that a numerology is a potent tool that you can always learn more about. I advise you to keep studying numerology if you want to go beyond reading your chart and truly delve deeper into the various numbers and how they can be interpreted in other ways. You'll probably be shocked to learn just how much there is to learn! To learn even more about yourself, you may start integrating your numerology practice with your astrology or tarot readings. You can even use numerology to help you develop a strong astrological or tarot reading routine.

The more time you devote to learning about yourself through hobbies like numerology, the simpler it will be for you to grow personally as you travel this path. It's critical to realize that tools like numerology should not be used as a strict rule book in your life, but rather as a guide. Keep in mind that, because you are a unique individual, there may be areas of your chart where you do not resonate as you read through and consider it. Pay attention to the areas where you resonate and don't be afraid to ignore the ones where you don't.

Going back to the double-digit number before the single-digit number may help you resonate even more deeply, allowing you to find an even deeper resonance. In other numbers, you might completely relate to the lead number and discover that it provides a wealth of information. In conclusion, numerology can teach you a lot about yourself, but the most important lessons come from meditating on it and observing how it applies to you in real life. You can discover more about yourself while also learning about numerology in this way.

Writing your chart down on paper or in a document will enable you to refer back to it whenever necessary. Many people discover that their charts become valuable to them at various points in their lives and frequently refer back to them. They can learn a lot about how to navigate different stages of life, what to anticipate from those around them, and how to make wiser decisions as a result. The biggest advantage of numerology is that you can move in alignment with your true soul by periodically reflecting on your chart.

The more you can align yourself with yourself through methods like numerology, the more balanced your life will be in the end. Understanding your habits and patterns is crucial in this situation since it will enable you to start making better-educated judgments once you have this knowledge at your disposal.

Numerology is about learning how to live in flow with yourself during this lifetime, not about being chained to a particular pattern or being "doomed" to a certain lifestyle.

Last but not least, if you liked this book, would you kindly take the time to leave an honest review on Amazon? We would value your opinion.

Many thanks, and have fun!

Describe the book

A numerology is a form of astrology that has been practiced since the late 500 B.C. This method of divination reading, which is thought to have been developed by the Greek philosopher Pythagoras, has been popular among the mystical community for many years. Anyone interested in learning more about numerology can find all the information they need in this practical guide.

For those who are completely new to fortune telling or for those who are interested in learning more about other occult practices like astrology or tarot, this book is a great resource. Despite being aimed at beginners, this book delves deeply into useful numerology knowledge so that you can finish feeling confident in your comprehension.

Grab a copy of Numerology for Beginners right away if you're eager to learn more about this spiritual practice and start learning more about yourself and the people you care about.

You will learn about the following topics in this book: What numerology is, how it functions, how you may read numbers Where numerology originated from and how it developed How contemporary numerology differs from historical numerology How to compute the various numbers in your chart

The meanings of the energies associated with each number; specific information about the numbers based on their placements; and what each number in your chart says about who you are. How to discover your more complex numbers, such as your secret skill or money number; How the numbers affect yearly cycles; What each yearly cycle signifies and what you will learn about it, numerology and reincarnation, the significance of your current incarnation for your future, and more!

www.ingramcontent.com/pod-product-compliance
Lightning Source LLC
LaVergne TN
LVHW020907200726
843506LV00011B/1599